TAROT FOR BEGINNERS

*A Step-by-Step Guide to Tarot Reading and Tarot Spreads
Using Tarot Cards*

VIVIENNE GRANT

CONTENTS

INTRODUCTION

When some people think of tarot reading, an image of that woman with weird-colored lipstick and scary eyes seated in a dimly lit room comes into mind. It's the kind of woman who seems to know more about you than yourself. That is not exactly true. Tarot reading should evoke images of a sacred place filled with peace and quiet where you can engage with the cards and understand yourself, your purpose, and your future better.

Although there is an increasing acceptance of tarot reading thanks to the internet, there are still many misconceptions out there. Some people take it as a way of knowing the future, magic, or the answer to everything, including finding a lost love or puppy. Tarot reading is simply an interesting way of using tarot cards to help you self-evaluate and seek answers. For a beginner, this may sound challenging, but relax—we will take this journey together.

In this guide, we will start in the past, looking at the history of tarot reading before observing the decks available. We will then look at cards in both the Major and Minor Arcana and what they mean before learning how tarot spreads and you can tarot read for yourself. Yes, I will be guiding you through your first reading! Isn't that exciting?

As this is a practical guide, this book will provide you with information that you can apply while on your tarot reading journey. You can be certain that by the end of this book, you will be in a position to tarot read successfully and obtain answers to those questions that may be causing you anxiety.

You no longer need to wonder if you can join the great world of tarot reading. The time is now, and the best resource to guide you through it is here. Welcome to the world of tarot reading, calmness, relaxation, open minds, great intuition, and the opportunity to predict the future and also take the necessary actions toward a better one.

Take a deep breath, relax your body, open your mind, and prepare to journey through the tarot world to a place of peace, knowledge, and better intuition.

The Tarot has become a widely known tool of divination, drawing many into its magic. However, the original purpose of the cards was not divination, but as a game. The first tarot cards trace back to the 14th Century in Europe. There are speculations that they came from Mamluk Egypt. Specifically the first records of such cards date back to 1367 in Berne before spreading to the rest of Europe. The European artists were the first to create these playing cards, featuring four different suits, similar to what is available in the modern world. The suits featured wands or staves, coins or discs, cups, and swords. In each suit, there were 14 cards, including ten pip cards, ranging from ace or one to ten. Additionally, the suit also included four face cards (page/Knave/Jake, Knight, Queen, and King.)

The ancestors of the game were mainly Italians

and the French; however, noting that the game of tarots likely originated from Egypt, the true ancestors are probably Egyptians. The Europeans receive much credit due to the better documentation in the area and widespread use of the game within the region, although different names were used to refer to the game. For instance, in France, it was the French Tarot, Italians had the tarocchini, while Australians called the game Königrufen. Many of these games are still in play to date across the world.

New Cards

Since humans are progressive in nature, after a few decades around 1440 and 1450, the Italians took the initiative of adding additional cards, which were painted with heavy allegorical illustrations and added to the existing suits. The earliest documented of these tarot packs were in Milan, Ferrara, Bologna, and Florence. People referred to the new decks as "triumph cards"—*carte da trionfi*—whereas the additional cards were simply called *trionfi*, or trumps for the English-speaking.

Unlike the standard triumph cards, the trump cards could be personalized. We all love to stand out and be unique, particularly the rich and mighty. The emergence of trump cards saw wealthy families and noble members of society commissioning artists to create unique cards for them.

The cards featured things or people that were important to them like family members, friends, and other interests. For instance, several sets that included various dukes and barons were made especially for the Visconti family in Milan. You may have come across them, since they still exist today.

The Visconti family was not alone; around 1420, Duke Fillippo Maria commissioned a 60-card deck. The delicate task was left in the hands of a painter named Michelino da Besozzo. Of the 60 cards, 16 were dedicated to Roman gods, whereas other suits depicted four types of birds.

In those early days, machines were limited, so the cards had to be painted by hand. If you wanted a set of cards, you had to have the means to hire a painter. If the design you chose was complicated,or you wanted a high quality of work done, then the painter had to be exceptionally good. Thus, having a customized set of cards was often reserved for the privileged few. Tarot cards became one way of showing social class.

Tarot Cards and the Printing Press

Like all things, the situation did not last. Humans, in a bid to make life easier and productive, invented the printing press. The printing press allowed for uniform printed matter to be produced in mass. Before the printing press, there was only a small number of cards, since the painters had to work on each one individually. However, with the ability to produce many cards in one go, the tarot cards became available to the wider population. The average player could enjoy a game of tarot without any wealth or titles.

Divination

Some people argue that using tarot cards for divination, at least playfully, goes back to the 14th century. In that era, Mamluk game cards from Turkey arrived in Western Europe. By the 1500s, the Italian aristocracy was playing a game called, *tarocchi appropriati*. In this game, random cards were dealt to the players, who then used the thematic associations on the cards to compose poetic verses about each other. Such predictive cards were known as *sortes*, meaning "lots" or "destinies." Up until this point, the cards were not often associated with predicting the future.

The earliest formally written work on the use of tarot words for divination is thought to have been in Italy and found in Marolino's Le Sorti around 1540. However, the most accepted was the Bologna in the 1700s. In Italy and France, tarot cards were a parlor game, and it was not until the late 16th and early 17th century that the tarot cards began to be associated with divination, although more simply. By the early 18th century, the divination of tarot cards began in earnest. People started to assign each card with a specific meaning. There were even those who offered suggestions on how to lay them out to meet the divinatory purpose.

By the mid-18th century, Italians were not the only ones with the mystical application for tarot cards; their divination had spread from Italy to other parts of Europe. French writer Antoine Court de Gébelin affirmed that tarot cards did originally come from Egypt and was founded in a holy book authored by Egyptian priests. The tarot was then introduced to Europe by African gypsies. Although this information was not entirely true, since Gypsies in Europe came from Asia and tarot came long before their arrival, it was still influential. Antoine linked the tarot to a mystical origin, giving a sort of basis on why many opted to use it for divination.

In 1791, Jean-Baptiste Alliette, a publisher and teacher, wrote a book on the tarot titled, *Etteilla*, or *the Art of Reading Cards*. Alliette further built on Antoine's assertion on the tarot being of Egyptian origin. He claimed that tarot cards were created with the Egyptians' legendary book of Thoth that was supposedly owned by the god of wisdom. Alliette further stipulated that the mystical book of Thoth was engraved into gold plates by the priests and provided the imagery for the earliest tarot deck.

. . .

The First Explicitly Divination Tarot Deck

Interestingly, it was Alliette who designed the first tarot deck specifically meant for divination around 1789. As expected, he used themes relating to ancient Egypt, keeping up with the belief that the cards originated from the book of Thoth. Alliette created his mystical pseudonym *Etteilla*, which is simply a reverse of his name.

Etteilla first learned the divination of tarot with a 32-card deck meant for a game called *Piquet* and added a special Etteilla card, referred to as the significator. The significator is a card that stands in for the person whose fortune is being read. Etteilla then switched to a traditional tarot deck for divination, as he believed that it held secret wisdom originating from ancient Egypt.

Etteilla was not alone. Many intellectuals in Europe during the late 18th century believed that writings and religion from ancient Egypt held important insights into the existence of humans. Thus, they were easily convinced that Etteilla knew what he was talking about. The link between the imagery on tarot cards and Egyptian mysticism gave them much credibility. With the intellectuals convinced of the mystic power associated with the tarot cards, it became easier for the advancement of use of tarot cards in divination. The strong backing by the intellectuals prompted increased interest from many quarters.

Interestingly, although Etteilla put in effort to

prove that the tarot cards were mystic, he still made their divination quite esoteric. Using information and the school of thought advanced by Antoine Court de Gébelin and his book, *The Primitive World*, he created a tarot deck that incorporated meanings into the suggestions from ancient Egypt. Unlike the earlier abstract interpretations and straightforward manner of reading that was associated with tarot in the 16th and 17th centuries, Etteilla introduced a deeper meaning to tarot.

Chapter Summary

In this chapter, we learned that:

- Tarot reading is thought to have originated from Egypt.
- Originally, it was a game until its use in divination caught on around the 18th century.
- The decks only became widely available after the introduction of the printing press.

In the next chapter, you will learn more about the modern deck, including what is available and what is best for you.

Interestingly, since those centuries ago when tarot cards started being linked to divination, there hasn't actually been much change. Look around you—every movie or series seems to have a mean, card-reading woman. Have you ever wondered why it is always a woman? Men also take part in card reading. Another interesting factor in those movies is the race of card bearing fortune tellers. Well, that aside, tarot cards' association with the mystical world has much to play in their appearances on our screens. The only difference is that the movie world portrays divination as dark and evil in most cases, instilling fear in others or giving the impression that it is a negative practice.

If you are one of those intimidated by tarot reading, you can breathe easy. There are no dark powers hiding within the cards and waiting to pounce on you. No, tarot cards are simply a deck of cards with words, numbers, and art printed on it. The art varies depending on the users and their culture or interests. Whatever is printed on the card only serves as symbols that can help people relate easily to their lives. Tarot cards are, therefore, tools that either remind us or represent things that we either want to attract to ourselves or let go from our lives.

Through tarot, you can come into a moment of introspection that can help to both heal and guide you toward a better life. Tarot gives you the opportunity to look closely within and address those deeply seated issues. You can pick a card and analyze what it means in order to find a solution. In a way, you do most of the work, but the cards walk the journey with you and make it seem like you are not really working.

With this understanding, you now know why there are differing decks around the world. People choose a deck that they can relate to and one they can interpret easily. If you look at the market today—be it in stores or online—you will be amazed by the high number of decks available. Did you know that there is even an emoji tarot deck? The world is advancing, and tarot is not left behind.

Inside the Modern Tarot Deck

Since the introduction of tarot in Europe and the rest of the world, the tarot deck has gone through various different designs. However, the modern and standard tarot deck includes 78 cards, each with its own divination meaning. The deck is divided into the major andMinor Arcanas. Of the 78 cards, 56 of them fall within theMinor Arcana, whereas the remaining 22 occur in the Major Arcana.

The Major Arcana

The Major Arcana includes the trump cards that are unsuited. Each card here represents a major force, hence the name "Major Arcana." When appearing in divination, a card from the Major Arcana ought to be taken seriously.

Every arcanum depicts a scene that either features a person or several of them and symbolic elements. In some decks, the cards have a name and a number although some in some decks, there are only pictures. Although the art may differ as per the deck, the symbolism is similar. Traditionally, the cards were not numbered, mainly due to illiteracy and how there was no standard order. Even then, there seemed to be an accepted order of the cards. For instance, the strength cards were the eleventh cards, while the Justice card was the eighth.

Since the order was not universally standardized, the introduction of the Rider-Smith deck saw a switch of the cards to create a better fit in correspondence to the Hermetic Order of the Golden Dawn. The Justice card took the eleventh position while The Strength card took the eighth position. The switch was adopted by many decks, more so those from the English-speaking world.

Cards found in the Major Arcana include: The Fool, The Magician, The High Priestess, The Empress, The Emperor, The Hierophant, The Lovers, The Chariot, Strength, The Hermit, Wheels of Fortune. Justice, The Hanged Man, Death, Temperance, The Devil, The Tower, The Star, The Moon, The Sun, Judgment, and The World.

The Minor Arcana

TheMinor Arcana's 56 tarot cards fall under four suits: Cups, Wands, Swords, and Pentacles or Coins. The four suits have 14 cards each, and each suit has a general meaning. Each card within the suit brings with it a unique message in divination.

Available Tarot Decks

The concept of the tarot deck is similar across the world, but people have preferences for different decks, depending on their ability to relate and interpret the cards. People have created different decks over time. Although some people keep just one deck their entire lives, others may have two or a dozen. There are even deck collectors who have as many as

1500 decks. That can give you an idea of how many different decks there are available. To give you some insight into the world of decks, let us look at some of the most common ones.

Rider-Waite Tarot Deck

If there was ever a title for the most popular tarot deck in the world, then it would certainly be the deck created by Pamela Colamn Smith and her husband, Arthur Edward Waite in 1909. Some people refer to the deck as Rider-Waite-Smith, Rider tarot deck, or Waite-Smith. Pamela, with her husband's guidance, made vibrant drawings that significantly transformed the standard tarot deck before its original publication by the Rider Company. The design of this deck was generally founded on the tenet of the Hermetic Order of the Golden Dawn. The images and symbols were influenced by Eliphas Levi, a 19th century occultist and magician.

Waite was a learned occultist. He put in much attention to detail, ensuring that all archetypal settings and possible symbols were part of the deck. His effort and spirit was echoed by Colman Smith, who not only worked on his instructions, but also added a sweet, artistic spirit. In the end, the images were not only full of details, but also beautiful and seemingly belonging to a wonderful fairytale.

Many people still refer to this deck as being timeless. Interestingly, the deck is suitable for card readers who are at the beginner or professional level. As a beginner, the Rider-Waite deck is highly recommended since it is rather friendly for beginners. Unlike most older decks, the Rider-Waite deck includes pictures on each card that depicts a situation or a sentiment, making it ideal for divination. Besides, the meanings are usually intuitive, and you can find resources on many of the descriptions about the meaning of tarot cards on this deck. Having this deck ensures that you are not entirely on your own and can look up help or clarification whenever possible.

The Wild Unknown Tarot Deck

Unlike the colorful Rider-Waite deck, the Wild Unknown comes mainly in black and white. The deck's personality embodies mystery and magic, making it ideal for divination. Don't be intimidated by its outright personality; this deck comes equipped with a well-detailed guidebook, making everything easy to understand. That is not all—the guidebook also contains some simple tarot spreads, the meanings of cards, and instructions, including how to shuffle the cards.

When beginning tarot, this would be an ideal deck for starting you off the ground with some instructions at hand. You only need to be aware of the naming of the cards, as the court cards have different names.

Mystic Monday Tarot Deck

Mondays are not only blue; in fact, in the world of tarot, they are mystic. The Mystic Monday deck is not meant for use on Mondays only, so don't be fooled by the name. The deck targets the modern tarot reader for whom it was designed. The depictions on the deck are bright and colorful with stunning, holographic edging.

In a way, it evokes interest, joy, and positive vibes while still striking a balance of colorful vibrancy and minimalism. If you would like to add some gist in your tarot reading, then the Mystic Monday deck is a good fit for everyday use. Many find this deck quite appealing, which has seen it being voted as one of the top decks out there

The Robin Wood Tarot Deck

If there was ever an intuitive deck, then it would be the Robin Wood Tarot deck. The design is done in a manner that makes the cards easy to read while also very intuitive.

Although the deck is not as traditional as the universal rider-waite, there are many people who connect to the images and find them easier to use. If you are not a fan of the rider-waite decks, then this will be the ideal deck to begin with. Easy to use, intuitive, and very descriptive.

The Modern Witch Tarot Deck

No, it does not turn you into a witch, nor does a witch appear. On the contrary, you may be immensely impressed by this deck, especially if you like the Rider-Waite one. Illustrated by Lisa Sterle, she brought in the traditional Rider-Waite's symbolism, fashionable, and youthful characters, while also including items from modern life. The deck makes it easier to relate to the cards, as they are inclusive and come with an air of fun and freshness.

The deck has impressive artwork with significant attention to detail, is solid to handle, and has thick and glossy cards. A small, white book also comes with the deck, and it is comprehensive and can help beginners navigate.

For beginners who do not want to go traditional and start from the ancient era, this is a good deck to begin with, as it contains items and illustrations that are easy to relate to for modern people.

The Radiant Rider-Waite Tarot Deck

As the name suggests, this deck was derived from the original Rider-Waite deck, but it is more radiant.

As a beginner, you will not only enjoy the cards' radiance, but the cards come with names written on them, unlike the traditional suit symbol and Roman numerals. Understandably, most people in the current generation face a real struggle dealing with Roman numerals, and hence, having names will likely be a better introduction to tarot. Besides, it will also help you build awareness of the cards and make easier connections.

Everyday Tarot Mini-Tarot Deck

The illustrations in the Mini-Tarot deck are simplified yet attractive and modern. In essence, this deck is based on the Rider-Waite scene, but is rather toned down, giving focus to some of the most fundamental symbols.

The advantage that this deck bears over many others and what makes it most ideal for beginners is its size. Being a mini-deck, you can take it anywhere, meaning you will also have easy access to them and can use them wherever you are.

Although this deck is not a favorite of most because of its thickness and the sticky gold trim that makes it hard to shuffle, it's great to use when studying the cards.

The Easy Tarot Deck

Another great beginner deck is the Easy Tarot Deck. Although it isn't as symbolically rich as other decks, it has quite a memorable illustration that can help you easily connect to the cards in the deck. The deck also comes with a book designed for learning to read tarot cards, which is particularly helpful for beginners.

What Is a Good Tarot Deck for Beginners?

We all have different tastes and preferences that affect our choices of tarot deck. However, as a beginner, some factors will make some decks more ideal than others. Before you reach for the most colorful, smallest, or even largest deck, remember that you will need more than that, for now. After gaining some experience in tarot reading, you will have a wider choice of decks to choose from.

When beginning, the deck you settle for must be suited for someone starting tarot reading. Ideally, a good beginner deck should be:

- **Rich in symbolism**—The deck should be symbolically rich with the scenes on the cards clearly established. You want to be able to interpret the cards intuitively, rather than memorizing keywords.
- **Aligned to common tarot descriptions**— During your first few days, you will likely

find yourself engaging in the internet and other resources for interpretations. Your choice of a tarot deck, therefore, needs to be one that is common and whose descriptions are easily found online. On the other hand, if your deck does not conform to the norm, you may get frustrated trying to find meanings and interpretations.

How to Choose Your Tarot Deck

You may already be overwhelmed by the sheer number of tarot decks available on the market and wondering how it is possible to choose one of these. Before you give up and wait for someone to give you the first deck or embark on a tarot deck shopping spree, here are some guidelines to help you narrow down your search. After all, since you have decided to start on tarot reading, there is no reason to hold back.

There is a common belief that your first set should be a gift, and you should not buy. However, why would you sit and wait until when someone *may* decide to get a tarot set for you? Go out and get it—I am here to help you get the ideal one.

- **Tarot decks are personal**

You may hear people rave about a certain deck like the Rider-Waite, and you may think it is the best— after all, it is considered universal. That is not reason enough, though; tarot decks are personal. The deck should speak to you in a language that you understand.

Look for cards that connect with you personally and intuitively. If you are browsing through decks online or looking at those in a store's display, feel the kind of energy they give you. Do you have a personal connection with the tarot deck?

If you find yourself using a deck and feeling frustrated or blank, then no matter the rave about it, it is not the deck for you. Your ideal deck will speak to you intimately. Trust your gut feeling!

- **Are you modern or traditional?**

Are you the type of person who is drawn to traditional things, or would you rather it be more modern? If you like the classic, traditional look and symbols, then you should settle for a deck like the original Rider-Waite or Tarot de Marseilles with symbols and illustrations from the ancient world. These are the ones with knights on a horse and soldiers with swords.

However, if you are more into modern looks with a typical affinity for contemporary things, then you should settle for a deck from this age, like the Fountain Tarot or Wild Unknown. With these decks, you will get symbols of a life that you can easily relate to, in addition to color, beauty, and elegance that can only come with time.

Ensure that your choice of deck appeals to you and the symbols are attractive and relatable.

- **Size matters**

There are different sizes of tarot decks. Like us, they come in all colors and sizes for you to choose from. There are tall cards, such as the giant tarot cards that are suitable for tarot readings for groups or parties. You certainly do not want to be carrying these around with you, however.

Many tarot decks come in the regular size, which will be perfect for home and personal use or face-to-face readings for clients. You will want the cards to be small enough to carry but also big enough to be visible and easy to handle.

There are also the small tarot decks—like the mini tarot deck—that can fit comfortably in a handbag. These are the kinds that you can take with you anywhere without worrying about space. Such cards will allow you to enjoy a tarot reading wherever you are, and they are ideal for traveling.

You may want to have different sizes of decks or settle for one; keep in mind the purpose of the deck. Another important factor to consider when choosing a size is the ability to shuffle the cards effectively. If the cards are either too small or too big, they may be difficult to shuffle. Hold the deck in your hand and feel how well you can handle it before purchasing.

- **The little white book**

Most decks come with a book that contains information on the artwork and tarot card meanings. Naturally, some decks will be generous with their details, whereas others will barely scratch the surface. Do not be surprised when some offer no information at all; the good news is that you can find much of the information online.

If you want to learn the meaning of a certain card, you can go through the white book that comes with the devk, which should tell you what it means and why. If the book is sketchy in detail, you can check online. You may also choose to interpret the cards based on your intuition.

Depending on how much information you want available in the little white book, you can choose a deck that will deliver what you are looking for.

- **The cards' imagery**

At the end of the day, tarot reading makes use of the images on the card, so take your time and go through the cards in detail. Exploring in this sense means going through the cards one by one. You can go online and look up as many images as possible. Ensure that you have seen each of them.

Assess the reactions you had to each image. Were you excited? Were you drawn to them? Ask yourself if you are drawn to the artwork and images. Do you find certain colors or patterns more appealing? In some instances, there are variations of a certain deck. Take a look at these and see which variation suits you better. For example, if you like brilliant decks you could choose the radiant Rider-Waite instead of the original Rider-Waite deck.

Remember that the focus of the tarot is deciphering the meaning of the cards, so take some time to explore the images in both the minor and Major Arcana. Ensure that you are getting some sense of meaning from them. Take for example how theMinor Arcana in the Tarot de Marseilles deck are different from the Rider-Waite in both imagery and story. In other decks, you will find that some cards are more visually appealing than others. Take the time to inspect the cards carefully. Having the right deck contributes to having a fulfilling, tarot-reading experience.

~

Quality Is Key

There is a high possibility that you will get attached to your deck. Some people prefer to use a certain deck all the time, whereas others have a special attachment to their first one. Whether you prefer different decks or are loyal to a particular one, you need to ensure you get quality.

Most tarot deck manufacturers provide cards with a good thickness, so you can use them for a long time. However, there are cheaper reproductions whose quality is compromised. They tend to tear easily or simply become damaged in a short time. Although it may be more expensive to get a high-quality deck, the return will be worth it. Invest in quality.

~

Buy Your Level

When you are a beginner, it is best to get a deck that is suitable for your level to avoid any frustration. You can opt for a deck like the Everyday Tarot Deck, which has clear and minimalist imagery, allowing you to connect with the symbols easily.

On the other hand, as you gain more experience, you may also get a bit bored with the beginner decks. You will need a challenge, since you will already have a good understanding of the standard cards. At such a time, you can opt for a deck like the Thoth deck, which is deeper and more complex. You can also settle for a mythical tarot deck—which will be abstract and much more challenging—such as the Shadowscapes Tarot.

Whatever your experience level, it is important to ensure that you connect with the cards and are comfortable with your deck's symbols and imagery.

Keep the Purpose in Mind

Tarot readings are for a wide variety of reasons, and your choice of a deck will depend on the readings you want to do, as well as how you intend to connect with them. For instance, if your purpose for tarot readings is to find some calm and peace in your world, then you can opt for the Osho Zen Tarot deck. If you wish to bond with your inner goddess, then the Goddess Tarot or Mythical Goddess Tarot will be more suitable.

The market offers a wide variety of tarot cards with different backgrounds and areas of focus. You can choose one depending on what works best for you. You could even have different decks, and that will be especially if you choose to go professional, so

you can attend to the needs of a diverse clientele or
your situation.

Chapter Summary

In this chapter, we have learned that:

- There are thousands of tarot decks
  available in the world.
- The Rider-Waite deck is the most widely
  used deck universally, and it is considered
  the king of tarot decks.
- For a beginner, the deck should be easy to
  understand and relatable.
- You can buy your first tarot deck—no need
  to wait for a gift.
- It would be best to get a tarot deck suitable
  for a beginner when starting out. Some
  decks to consider include the Radiant
  Rider-Waite Tarot deck, Everyday Tarot
  Mini Tarot Deck, and Easy Tarot Deck,
  among others.
- You should connect with your deck
  personally and intuitively.

In the next chapter, we will look into tarot decks more deeply, dissecting the meaning of each card so you can be well-prepared for tarot reading. The aim is to give you a good start on what each card stands for as you experience and learn about the magic of tarot reading.

CHAPTER 3

MEANING OF TAROT CARDS—
THE MAJOR ARCANA

Have you bought a tarot deck that truly tantalizes your soul? If not, at least have an idea of what to buy or look out for when shopping. No pressure though; there is no hierarchy in tarot decks. You would simply listen to your intuition and go with the one that you feel is the one. The good news is that you won't be entering an eternal covenant; you can also choose something else.

Well, since you are equipped with either the deck or information on the deck, it is time to understand what exactly is contained in it. You are also aware that the standard tarot deck contains 78 cards, 22 of which are in the Major Arcana and 56 are in the Minor Arcana. Let us explore what these cards stand for and their meanings.

First, it is important to note that tarot divination was founded on the Hermetic truism that, "as above, so below." Hence, the macrocosm of the universe is mirrored in that of the individual experience; one tarot deck contains the entire universe. Each card represents a place, person, or event. Therefore, the division of the cards into major and Minor Arcanas is a reflection of the occurrences in a person's life. Although the Major Arcana cards speak to great secrets, theMinor Arcana cards speak to small secrets.

Both the Minor and the Major Arcana cards make a comprehensive, illustrative language that gives snippets into our lives. Since the deck is a representation of the whole world, all the answers to questions we ask exist within the deck. Each card stands for a circumstance, person, or potential outcome. The good news is that you can expect tarot reading to be an open book with no secrets, hidden agendas, or puzzles. Everything depends on your capacity to discern the meaning of the symbols within your own interpretation. Your intuition plays the key role in tarot reading.

In this section, we will evaluate each card and their meaning to ensure that you are in a position to interpret them correctly.

The Major Arcana

Containing 22 cards, the Major Arcana is the foundation and core of the tarot deck. Though the entire tarot deck has archetypal meaning, the significance is very pronounced within the Major Arcana. All major events in your life appear within the Major Arcana.

The Major Arcana is typically a story of the spiritual travels observed from the innocent wonder of the Fool, who goes on to reach the fulfilment of the world. In essence, the Major Arcana tells the story of the spiritual evolution of humanity into individuation and enlightenment. As you embark on the journey with the Fool, you will realise common parallels between your life stages and those in the cards. Each card teaches a particular life lesson, which will be a certain concept to meditate. Some readings are done using only the Major Arcana.

Let us look at the 22 cards that make up this Arcana in detail to increase your understanding of these crucial cards.

The Fool

We consider being a fool as a negative in life. However, it is not always the situation, at least not for tarot reading. When you have your first tarot reading you are considered to embody a fool. If you look keenly at the Fool tarot card, you will see a young person carrying a small sack and walking joyfully, exuberantly, and excitedly into the world. His small sack shows that he cares little about the possible dangers ahead.

However, the danger is imminent; if he takes one step, he will topple over the cliff, which is the same one he is reaching. That does not seem to bother him at all, which implies that he is either naïve or unaware. He has a dog barking in a warning and prompting his need to be more aware of his environment before he plunges to his fall, killing all his dreams and hopes for adventure.

In numbered decks, the Fool is number 0, showing infinite potential and a blank slate. You may want to laugh at the fool, but at the first reading, he will be whom you embody. Conversely, the fool is the wisest person in this world; he is the one who knows everything. The Fool here represents the eternal soul and is also the symbol of enlightenment. Interestingly, it is both the first and the last trump card in the deck, signifying a cycle, as is life. The Fool symbolizes a free spirit, the inner child, innocence, and new beginnings.

When reversed, the Fool represents what a fool is known for in the modern world; recklessness and being taken advantage of. At the same time, he portrays a spirit of risk-taking and courage. He reminds you that there are opportunities to open up your life to new areas, which comes with awe, curiosity, wonder, and anticipation, but you can never really know what lies ahead; you can only take everything with positivity and joy.

The Magician

Most of us have a complicated relationship with magicians. They are exciting when in a show, but when it gets personal, we get skeptical. Looking at this tarot card, you can see the person holding the hand with the wand up to the sky, whereas the other hand points downwards. He seems to be affirming that, "as is above, so below." It is also a reflection of the outer world reflecting within, and Earth reflecting God. In his position of giving presence to things above and those below, the magician card also symbolizes his capacity to act as an intermediary between the human world and that above.

Let us focus on his table. There lies all the tarot suits symbolizing the four elements: water, air, fire, and earth. The presence of the tarot suits shows that magicians connect these elements.

One of the more interesting and inspiring aspects about the Magician is the infinity sign on his head. Infinity means endless, and in this case, it presents unending possibilities of what is achievable if you have the will.

In essence, the magician represents pure willpower. Using the power of the elements of water, earth, air, and fire, and that of the suits, the innate potential in the Fool is moulded into the power of desire. He learns to want things so bad that he does not let anything discourage him. As the connecting force between this world and the above, he brings to the fore that the mind is a reflection of the world and vice versa. What the magician says is that you are powerful, and with your willpower, you can create an ideal inner world, and the outer world will follow suit.

Getting a Magician reading shows that it is time to believe in yourself and tap into your full potential with confidence. The Magician card is a wakeup call to take action in whatever sphere of your life, knowing that you have the potential to undertake anything, and you should take advantage of the existing opportunity. Make a progressive choice that will come with great changes.

When you land on the reversed Magician tarot card, it shows an illusion. The Magician has power, but he is also the master of illusions. He can be tricky and deceptive, easily luring you by his showmanship while manipulating you for selfish gains. Consider the reversed magician as a warning that someone in your circle pretends to care and advance your interests when it is not true. It is a call to know the people around you very well before trusting them. Additionally, it could also act as a caution that your obsession with power may cause you to make wrong and reckless decisions that could be the cause of your downfall.

The High Priestess

The High Priestess sits tall between two pillars at the temple of Solomon, Jachin, and Boaz. Boaz, found on the left, is referred to as the Pillar of Strength, whereas the one on the right is Jachin, also known as the Pillar of Establishment. The two pillars show how dual life is. For example there is feminine and masculine, positive and negative, and good and evil.

If you look at this card, you will note that the High Priestess sits right between the two pillars, indicating that she has a role to play in mediating the dualities of life. She holds the position of the third pillar and allows for a path between the dualities of life. She is accomodative to their existence and understands there is knowledge to be gained from both worlds. On her head is the crown of Isis, showing that she believes in magic. The solar cross that she wears is an indication of her connection to the earth and its element. On her feet is a crescent moon, similar to one associated with the Virgin Mary. The moon shows that she has a hold over her emotions, whereas the pomegranates denote her ambition.

You have to acknowledge the calm assurance that comes with the High Priestess that is only associated with someone who has a wealth of inner knowledge. She exudes confidence and calmness. Landing on the High Priestess card in a reading calls for you to stop, calm down, and listen to your intuition over your conscious mind or intellect. The High Priestess card can also depict divine feminine, which is the characteristic of a person linked to intuition, sensuality, creation, community, and collaboration. The feminine energy also comes with a warrior spirit and deep sense of both balance and justice. She is a representation of someone who is intuitive and ready to open up to her spirituality. The setting on the card is night time, meaning that the world may be frightening, but she can lead you into growth.

The High Priestess symbolizes psychic energy, the unconscious, instincts, feelings, and emotions. She is aware of what is brewing below the surface while still being a receptive mirror. She is the connection to the instinctual powers. Her appearance in a reading calls for you to listen to her message and search within yourself for the answers you seek; the answers lie within.

The Empress

The Empress is a beautiful woman who exudes a peaceful and grounded aura. She has blonde hair and wears a crown with twelve stars on her head that depict a connection with the natural cycles, which are the twelve planets and twelve months of the year. The crown also indicates that she is connected to the mystical realm. She stands for fertility, as denoted by her robe with patterns of pomegranate and her sitting on luxurious cushions embroidered with a sign of Venus—the planet of love, fertility, creativity, grace, and beauty. Venus rules her world, meaning that there is complete harmony. Love, luxury, and fertility all occur by the grace of this goddess.

From her throne, abundant nature surrounds her, including an enchanting lush forest with a river streaming, a depiction that this woman is the representative of the Earth Mother archetype and the goddess of fertility. She brings blessings and abundance. She derives her sense of peace from her environment, the water, and the trees, enjoying the rejuvenating energy of nature. The foreground of the card shows golden wheat, which is a reflection of a recent abundance which signifies abundance.

As you can already tell, the Empress is a strong, peaceful character that depicts a connection with femininity. In this sense, femininity includes sensuality, creative expression, elegance, fertility, and nurturing—all qualities that are crucial in maintaining a balance between the genders. Landing on an Empress card is a call to get in touch with your feminine energy and create some beauty in life. The Empress asks you to connect with your sense of touch, sound, sight, and smell to experience deep fulfillment and pleasure.

Oftentimes, we ignore our environment and the

simple pleasures of life, like enjoying quiet time listening to the sound of water or the fresh breath of air. The Empress is a sign that you can use your sensuality to attract life circumstances that bring joy and happiness, be kind to yourself, and take time to take care of you. Enjoy some good food, go for a massage, and discover new ways of expressing yourself like painting, drama, or music. You could even take up a new hobby.

The Empress is also a sign of abundance, meaning that you have everything you need to enjoy a comfortable life. You are now in a growth period where things are working out, and you are seeing fruits. An Empress tarot reading is an opportunity to be grateful for the bounty and continue to build on the energy to achieve even more.

That is not all—the Empress is a strong depiction of pregnancy and motherhood. Not only does it point to an actual pregnancy, but it could also mean the birth of something new, such as a business, idea, or project. You can take this card as an indication of good fortune and success that is due to you.

Being the archetype of Mother Earth, the Empress encourages you to venture outdoors, enjoy nature, ground your energy, and get into a rhythm with the flow of the Earth. Take a walk, go to the beach, forest, or lake and appreciate the beauty that nature has to offer. Let your mind be at ease, allowing yourself to enter into a relaxed frame of mind and receive nature's grounding spirit. Like the Empress, you will be in a place to nurture and care for others, offering love, compassion, and support.

Reversed Empress

When you land on the Reversed Empress card, it's a sign that you are placing too much effort on other people's affairs and losing much of your willpower. You may be taking the empress' role over-board, nurturing others too much and neglecting yourself. Alternatively, it could also indicate that you are too reliant on others to care for you and even make your decisions. The Empress is calling to your attention the need to take care of your matters, remove deep external influence, and build confidence to solve matters by yourself.

The Emperor

Having met tarot's mother, the Empress, there is an implication that there is a father somewhere. Meet the Emperor—the Father archetype of Tarot, who is a stoic figure seated on a large stone throne. His head is adorned with heads of four rams, a sign of affiliation with the astrological sign, Aries. He sits upright, confident, and exuding a sense of leadership. The sceptre, ankh, in his hand represents his right to rule and reign, and it is also a symbol of life, as per Egyptian culture. The orb held in the other hand symbolizes the kingdom he is in charge of. He wears his beard long, which is a sign that has gained much experience over the years. He knows what it takes to be a ruler, establish authority and power, and maintain order for the sake of the people. His red robe is a sign of passion, power, and energy for life. The suit of armor he wears under the robe is a suggestion that he is under protection from threats, while the gold crown makes him an authority—someone who has to be heard.

Looking at his background, you can see the barren mountains that are in contrast with the lush and greenery of the Empress. The barren mountains depict his ambition and determination to conquer greater heights and improve his capacity as a leader. They also signify a solid foundation and resistance to making any unnecessary change. Unlike the nurturing nature of the Empress, the Emperor rules with strength, force, and grit. However, the presence of a small river beneath the surface indicates that there is a hidden soft side to the emperor—one that requires much digging.

The Emperor card symbolizes regulation, authority, fatherliness, and organization. He is a strategic thinker who follows his plans through while being the symbol of masculine principles. Landing on this card means that you take up the paternal responsibility of ensuring a structure, establishing systems and rules, and imparting knowledge. You take up the role of providing, protecting, and defending the people you love. You are their rock, offering security and stability.

Like the Emperor—as a representation of a powerful leader—this card shows that you like power, status, and recognition. You like being in a position of leadership where you direct and command others, ruling with a hand that is firm but fair. While you listen to others, you reserve the right to have the final say and thrive amidst conflicts. You will do everything to protect your loved ones, and they, in turn, offer respect and loyalty.

The emperor works within rules and regulation. Picking this card shows that you apply guidelines and principles to situations, creating an environment bound by law and order. You have the ability to walk into a chaotic situation and create calmness by being strategic, systematic, and highly organized. The card also depicts experience gained over the years and a considerable level of expertise. You are now in a position to offer guidance and direction to others. You can make a change because you know that to reign means to serve. By lifting others, you make a positive difference. The Emperor always acts for the greater good of his people.

Reversed Emperor

On the flip side, the Reversed Emperor indicates an abusive authoritarian power. The Emperor can be rigid and domineering; a reversed Emperor reading can display an overuse or abuse of power, either from you or someone around you, like a supervisor, partner, or father figure. The situation can also arise from childhood insecurities. You need to ask yourself if you are asserting so much power that you leave others powerless, or if you are allowing others to have too much power and authority over you.

Another possible indication of the Reversed Emperor that you could be shying away from taking up a leadership role that others expect of you. Instead of being the leader you are expected to be, you could be hiding away in the shadows. It is time to stand up and make a difference by doing things that have an impact, such as training or even writing a book. On the other hand, if you are feeling overwhelmed by an abusive person, it is time to stand up to them. Call out the bullies, inefficient system, or unhealthy environment. Looking strategically—it may be time to become your own boss or leave a toxic relationship.

If you are struggling to get things done, the Reversed Emperor card could indicate that it is time to evaluate your commitment to your plans and goals. You may need to get a bit tough on yourself and your team members to deliver results.

∾

The Hierophant

As the High Priestess is female, the Hierophant is male. His other names include the Pope, the Teacher, and the High Priest. Taurus rules here.

Like the High Priestess, he sits between two pillars, although his temple is different from hers. On his head lies a three-tiered crown, and he wears three robes: red, white, and blue, which represent the three worlds under him—the superconscious, conscious, and subconscious. You will notice the papal cross in his hand, which shows that he holds a high religious status. The three horizontal bars in the cross are known to represent the three Godheads: the Father, the Son, and the Holy Spirit. His right hand is raised in a religious blessing. Two of his fingers point toward the Earth, while the other two point toward Heaven.

There are two acolytes beneath him that indicate knowledge transfer within institutions. The Hierophant's main task is to ensure that spiritual wisdom is passed down to others, and they are initiated into the institution where they can take up some roles. The two acolytes in the card show a path to education and knowledge. Looking around his feet, you can see the crossed keys that portray a balance between the subconscious and conscious minds, as well as the unlocking of mysteries that only the Hierophant can teach.

Upright Hierophant

If you land on this card, it suggests that you wish to follow the established and conventional processes. You desire to take the orthodox approach instead of being innovative. The Hierophant card calls for you to understand, follow the established social structures, and be part of processes and ceremonies. You can consider this as a sign to conform to the current set of rules and culture. You can also take up formal learning to improve your expertise.

Since the Hierophant is associated with religion and spiritual beliefs, the card suggests that before you embark on discovering your belief systems and making choices, it is best to take some time to learn the basic principles. Find an authority, mentor, or teacher to guide you through spiritual beliefs and values to nurture your awareness in that area.

If, on the other hand, you have mastered a certain field, this card suggests taking up a teaching and mentoring role. You acknowledge and honor your responsibility in transferring education and knowledge to others in a structured manner, as such has existed over different generations.

Additionally, the Hierophant card calls for membership in social groups or institutions, which comes with a sense of comfort and belonging. Having people with a well-established belief system and explicit values is an asset to any individual. You can achieve this by joining a church, gym, or even tarot community. The goal is to identify with people with whom you share a way of thinking and those who inspire further learning.

Reversed Hierophant

The Reversed Hierophant is a reminder that you are the teacher, and any knowledge that you pursue comes from within. The card urges you to forge your path and find your set of beliefs instead of following others blindly. Although doing so may be challenging and even unsettling at first, you will, over time, learn to tap into your inner knowledge and gain confidence. In essence, the reversed Hierophant tells you that you can do things on your own without the need for external approval.

The card could also mean that it is time to challenge the status quo. You have different world views and are ready to test what has been advanced to you as the truth. You can seek out other opportunities that can help you reclaim your power. If you have been feeling constrained or restricted, it is time to find your sense of flexibility and freedom by making your rules. The reversed Hierophant encourages you to evaluate the standard way of doing things and see if it aligns with your inherent beliefs and values. However, the situation could also result in conflict with those in authority.

The Lovers

The Lovers card shows an image of a naked man and woman standing beneath an angel, Raphael, the angel of air. Air is linked to mental activity—to be specific, communication, which is the founding principle of healthy relationships. The name "Raphael" also means "God heals." The zodiac sign is Gemini.

The angel seems to be blessing and protecting them, a reminder that their union is divine. A sense of security and happiness abounds in their home, the Garden of Eden, as depicted by the fruit tree and the snake. There is more to the fruit tree with the snake than simply showing location; drawn from the biblical story of the Garden of Eden, the snake and fruit trees tell of the fall of humanity into temptation.

The serpent and fruit refer to the sensual pleasures that may take your focus away from what is divine. There is a tree of flame right behind the man that represents passion, which is what concerns men the most. The twelve flames depict all the zodiac signs, symbolizing time and eternity.

The man is looking at the woman, who in turn looks at the angel, indicating a path of the consciousness from the conscious to subconscious, and then to the superconscious. It is a reflection of a path from physical desires to emotional needs and on to concerns on spiritual matters.

There is a volcanic mountain within the background of the Lovers card, which is rather phallic and can be viewed as a depiction of passion that erupts when a man and woman come together in full nudity.

Upright Lovers

The card stands for attractiveness, perfection, and harmony in a relationship. The couple has unity and trust that gives them strength and confidence, which is empowering and creates a strong bond. The two could be closely related, either in marriage or any other intimate relationship. Upright lovers depict meaningful relationships and conscious connections. If you get this card in a tarot reading, it means that you have a great, soul-honoring, and beautiful connection with someone. For instance, your search for a soulmate is over, or the connection you have with someone is beyond instant gratification to being spiritual. The focus of this card is not only on romantic relationships, but also on meaningful relationships with respect, love, and compassion.

Away from the seemingly obvious meaning, the Lovers card also indicates a choice between opposing forces. You may be in a dilemma, like the couple in the cards, drawn by physical desires and temptations, while they can focus on the joy in the garden, protection accorded to them, and spiritual matters. Similarly, you could be in a situation that calls for you to examine and choose your best course of life. Although it may be tempting to choose what meets your burning desires, it may be best to choose the right path for a lifetime.

Both the man and woman are naked, meaning there is raw honesty and open communication. It thus tells you of the need to communicate openly in your relationship to make it more fulfilling and harmonious, full of respect and trust.

Reversed Lovers

The Reversed Lovers card points to internal and external conflicts and the disharmony that can make life difficult and puts undue pressure on relationships. With this card, think about whether you are punishing yourself for the things that you can fix or let go of easily. Ensure that your personal beliefs and values are aligned with the kind of life that you want.

The card could also suggest a communication breakdown between you and your partner. The unity that exists in the relationship—like in the card—due to open communication is missing. The situation puts a strain on the relationship.

Alternatively, it could indicate that you are avoiding responsibility. You may have chosen gratification of your desires and the consequences are catching up, yet you blame others and refuse to acknowledge the mistake. The time to make amends is now, and like the Lovers, forge a path from physical desires to emotional needs, and on to spiritual matters. You need to gear up for growth, and it comes with responsibilities.

∼

The Chariot

This card shows a warrior inside a chariot driven by two sphinxes: a black and a white one. On his shoulders is a sign of a crescent moon that indicates his coming into being or the spiritual influence that guides him. His tunic has a square that denotes the element of the earth and material things grounding him, as well as possession of the strength of will. The other alchemical symbols represent his spiritual transformation. The star crown and laurel on his head show that he is enlightened of pure will, successful, and victorious. Although riding in a chariot, he does not hold any reins, symbolizing that his control comes from his mind and will. There is a canopy of six-pointed stars above him, giving him a connection to the divine and celestial world.

The black and white sphinxes indicate duality and opposing forces that exist in the journey, and the charioteer has to be in control of them. Although they appear calm, they scuffle, indicated in how they are looking in different directions. The charioteer, therefore, has to ensure that the sphinxes go in a certain direction using his sheer resolve and willpower. A wide river flows in the background, symbolizing the need to flow with life's rhythm while working on one's goals. The zodiac sign for this card is Cancer.

Upright Chariot

The upright chariot talks of determination, strength, and willpower. The focus here is on overcoming challenges and being victorious by retaining control of your surroundings. Using willpower and strength when faced with obstacles is critical in achieving one's goals. Thus, you must be confident, focused, and determined through a process that is filled with detours and winding turns. If you have a set goal or plan in place, you should pursue it as orderly as possible, with structure. Keep your eye on the goal.

The Chariot is a sign of encouragement, telling you that success is yours if you stay focused, assert yourself, and put away self-doubt. You have to be confident in your abilities and bold in your plans. You may experience some odd behaviors with yourself, like competitiveness and aggression. Although these are natural and useful in pursuing your goals, you must rein them so they do not hinder your progress.

Reversed Chariot

If you land on a Reversed Chariot Card, take a look at yourself. You may be lacking in willpower, motivation, focus, and direction. You could also be so obsessed with achieving your goals that you are becoming too aggressive. The Reversed Chariot is telling you that you cannot be in control all the time, and you need to accept all other factors that are also in play.

The reversed chariot also shows a lack of direction and control in your life. When faced with the opposing forces and obstacles, you are unable to muster the strength to handle them. Without determination and direction, life throws you around as it pleases. You, therefore, have to wake up and make bold choices and decisions that can change your destiny and take you to where you want to go.

Strength

When they talk about the strength of a woman, the woman in question must be the one in this card. Here she is, in all her grace, holding a lion and petting it as if it were a cat. With a calming and loving energy, she tames a creature known for its ferociousness, going as far as stroking its forehead and jaw. She displays courage by holding its jaws. She appears calm and collected with full confidence that the lion is under her dominion. The lion symbolizes raw passions and desires, and the woman shows that with resilience and inner strength, knowing that the animal instinct can be tamed. She represents being in control and calm when faced with great adversities. Instead of using force or coercing the lion, she uses her inner strength to control and subdue the lion, displaying love and compassion.

The woman is wearing a white robe that stands for her pure spirit. The belt and crown made of flowers is the most beautiful and fullest expression of nature. Even the universe agrees with her way of doing things. The blue background appearing over the mountains depicts calmness and stability. She has a symbol of infinity on her head that represents her infinite wisdom and potential.

Upright Strength

If you land on the Strength card, you can do a happy dance. The card indicates that you possess inner strength, power, determination, and courage, even during times of distress and danger. The Strength card is similar to the Chariot, except that it focuses on inner strength and a spirit able to over-come obstacles. You can remain strong and calm, even when undergoing challenges and struggles. In all that, you retain your compassionate nature, allo-cating time for others even at your inconvenience. Your strength comes from knowing that you can endure the obstacles life throws at you due to stamina, persistence, inner calm, and patience. You commit to your undertakings and go about your tasks in a composed and mature manner.

The Strength card also shows that you do not rule

or lead by controlling or coercing others, but rather through persuasion and influence. You have inner strength, strong will, determination, and personal power. People may underestimate your power as being invisible, but you can control a situation quietly without excessive force. You can also overcome fears and doubts. Getting the Strength card encourages you to tame any animal instincts, raw emotions, and passions that you may have and respond constructively to them.

Reversed Strength

A reversed Strength card calls for you to examine your level of confidence and inner strength. These levels could be too high or too low, and you need to bring them into balance. The card could also mean that you are in a period of fear or anger with little memory of what being passionate and confident felt like. You could also be feeling some depressive thoughts and enjoying very little happiness from life. You must learn to reclaim control of your life and become confident again in your abilities to regain your inner strength.

∾

The Hermit

The Hermit card displays an old man standing by himself at the peak of a snow-capped mountain. The snow-capped range denotes growth, development, accomplishment, success, and spiritual mastery. The Hermit chose a path of self-discovery and success-fully achieved a heightened awareness state. He has achieved spiritual knowledge and is ready to share his knowledge with others. He is committed to his path and fully cognisant of his choice.

On one hand, he holds a lantern containing a star with six points, which is the seal of Solomon and symbolizes wisdom. The lantern illuminates his way but is limited to the area around him. To see further, he must keep going. Everything is not revealed at once; rather, it is in small bits as he continues on his chosen path. In his left hand, he has a long staff that he uses for balance; it is a sign of authority and power.

Upright Hermit

The Hermit card depicts a seeker of knowledge and a person willing to detach from the crowd, find peace and solitude, and discover his inner voice and listen to it. He understands the need for stillness, a disconnection from voices, desires that threaten his search, and the need to focus on a path through his unconscious to self-discovery.

The Hermit card affirms the importance of taking a break from the hustle and bustle of life to draw your attention and energy inward and find the answers you search from deep within. You have to tap into yourself to discover the most profound knowledge and truth. Landing on this card affirms that now is the ideal time to take that weekend retreat in a quiet place or go on a sacred pilgrimage. You need to take time off to contemplate your values, motivations, and principles and find your authentic self.

The Hermit appears at a time in your life when you are considering taking a new direction. The card tells you to contemplate, meditate, and undertake careful self-examination on what your goals and dreams entail before making a decision. By looking at your life with deep and spiritual understanding, you will change your priorities and general direction for the better.

You can also consider this card as a call to shy away from being part of the materialistic or consumerist society and instead concentrate on yourself and your inner world. Additionally, it could indicate that it is time to raise your spiritual vibrancy and improve your consciousness by looking within for answers.

Reversed Hermit

When you land on the Reversed Hermit, it could be an indication that you need to take more time for personal reflection. On the other hand, it could also mean that you are taking too much time for self-discovery. If you are not spending enough time on meditation and personal reflection, it is time to create some space and do some soul-searching on rebuilding your spiritual level.

If you are already allocating much time to reflecting and meditation, the reversed Hermit is a wake-up call not to take isolation too far. You should not forget about the importance of connections with others, even as you discover and stay in touch with your inner self. As a person, you have responsibilities to others. Do not get so wrapped up in your journey that you neglect your loved ones.

The Wheel of Fortune

The Wheel of Fortune is a highly-symbolic card, with each symbol carrying its own meaning. The card has a giant wheel at its center with esoteric symbols. Different creatures including an eagle, bull, lion, and angel surround the wheel, depicting the zodiac signs of Taurus, Scorpio, Aquarius, and Leo. They also symbolize the four evangelists found in Christian tradition, which may be why they are adorned with wings. The wings on the creatures also represent stability amidst change and movement. Interestingly, each of them holds a book, the Torah, signifying wisdom and self-understanding.

On the edges of the wheel are three creatures. On the left side is a snake that seems fast on the descent. The snake is a sign of the god of evil Typhon found in ancient Egypt and symbolizes a plunge into the material world. The Anubis—the Egyptian god of the dead—rises on the right side of the wheel, welcoming souls into the underworld. A sphinx sits on the top part of the wheel, symbolizing strength and knowledge. The Anubis and the sphinx appear to be a rotating cycle, ensuring that as one goes up, the other comes down.

The wheel's face has the Hebrew letters YHVH inscribed on it, which stand for the unpronounceable God's name. There are also the letters TORA, considered to be a version of the word Torah, meaning law. In the middle of the wheel are the alchemical symbols for sulphur, water, salt, and mercury. These are the building blocks for both the four elements and life. They are a symbol of formative power.

Upright Wheel of Fortune

The wheel of fortune is a reminder that life is constantly changing and nothing is permanent. If you are in a difficult phase, you can be sure that the wheel will move and it will pass. Similarly, if things are going very well for you, remember that it will also pass, and you will find yourself back to "normal" or undergoing some challenges. Thus, it is important to cherish the good times in life and make the most out of them; they could be gone any minute.

The wheel also symbolizes karma—"what goes around comes around." You have to bear in mind that if you are good to others, they will also be good to you, but if you treat people badly, they will also treat you terribly in turn. The good that you send out to others is what the Universe will send back to you. Moreover, the card encourages you to be willing to receive help from others. Embrace support from both the spiritual and physical realms.

If you have a high preference for control and stability, landing on the wheel of fortune cards suggests that external factors are influencing your position and situation. There is no longer a surety of processes and the universe is giving you what it pleases. You should prepare for unpredictable and unnerving situations. You have to be willing to accept what is handed to you and adapt. On the other hand, the wheel of fortune could also mean a turning point in your life. You may find yourself accessing opportunities you never thought possible. You now have a chance to make significant changes, find a new direction, and better your life.

Reversed Wheel of Fortune

When reversed, the Wheel of Fortune is an indicator that you may experience bad luck and unexpected negative changes. You need to realize that this is not up to you, but due to external forces. You, however, have a choice to sit around moping about it or getting up on your feet and getting your life back on track. Besides, you can be sure that the wheel will turn again.

Justice

Like the High Priestess and the Hierophant, the figure of Justice sits between two pillars symbolizing law, structure, and balance. In front of her is a loosely hanging purple veil, symbolizing compassion. She is a symbol of truth, law, and fairness.

In her right hand is a sword that represents her

logical and organized mindset, which is integral to the fair dispensation of justice. If you look at the sword, you will note that it is upward-facing, depicting a firm and final decision, while its double-edged blade is a reminder that your actions attract consequences. In her left hand is a scale, which is a sign of her impartiality and a pointer that intuition should always balance with logic. She wears a crown on her head with a small square on it that depicts her well-ordered thoughts. On her feet, a white shoe appears from under her garments as a reminder that actions also have spiritual consequences.

Upright Justice Meaning

The Justice card symbolizes truth, fairness, justice, and the law. The decisions you take now have consequences for you and others in the long term. You have to account for your actions and accept being judged accordingly. If you have acted fairly and for the greater good, you can relax, knowing that you can expect only goodness. If not, then you have to be ready to deal with the consequences of your actions. Well, it is not all bleak, even for those unfair and unjust people. The Justice card comes accompanied with a level of understanding and compassion, which allows for fairness.

If you are in a situation of seeking justice, you can take landing this card as a positive sign that you will get what you seek. When the judgment is passed, take it and move forward; the Justice card is final with no retrials. However, if you have wronged another, consider this card as a warning that can allow you to make things right and change into a better version of yourself.

If you find that you need to make an important decision or choice, be careful and bear in mind the consequences that your decision will have on you and others. Balance your intuition with logic and choose the path that offers the greatest good for all. Remember that you are responsible for the actions you take, and you have to stand by your decision.

The upright justice card also depicts truth based on facts that must always come to pass. Always strive to learn the truth before passing judgment. This card is a call to be fair in all your dealings, and if there is an area in your life that needs attention, or you are uncertain, you must take action. You must ensure that you get a sustainable solution.

Reversed Justice

A Reversed Justice card in tarot reading could indicate that your life is in denial. You are unwilling to accept and deal with the consequences of your actions, evading guilt and not remedying the situation. You can rest assured that those actions are in the past, and today offers an opportunity to do the right thing and make things better. Although taking action now may not take away the occurring consequence, it will help you stop judging yourself.

The Hanged Man

He hangs upside down from the living world tree, seeing the world from a different perspective. Despite his hanging, he has a calm and serene facial expression that suggests he is hanging there by choice. Although his right foot is bound to the tree, his other leg is free. He bends it at the knee and tucks it behind his bound leg. Similarly, his arms are also bent, with his hands held behind his back to form an inverted triangle.

He wears red pants, a symbol of human passion and the physical body. His shirt is blue, a color that depicts calm emotions, knowledge, and one that is associated closely with saints. On his feet are yellow shoes that represent his intelligence. There is a halo on his head, displaying awareness, new insights, and enlightenment.

The Hanged Man shows ultimate surrender, sacrifice, martyrdom, and being suspended in time.

Upright Hanged Man

The position of the Hanged Man is a sacrifice that is necessary for making progress in life. You could be repenting for past wrongs or simply taking a step back to re-evaluate how you would like to move forward. The time you spend hanging upside down, calm, and looking at things from a different perspective is not wasted; rather, it is quality time spent finding the right path.

The card reflects a need not to rush decisions, but suspend decision making for a certain period. Such a move will give you some time to weigh the situation and assess it from all views before making any critical decisions. The Hanged Man suggests that waiting in suspension may be the key to achieving success, or it could merely give you time for the right opportunity to appear. Sometimes, a failure to act is the solution to challenges you are facing.

In a tarot reading, the appearance of the Hanged Man may indicate that some of your activities and projects are coming to an abrupt or unexpected halt. Instead of burning energy pushing them forward, take it as a chance to re-assess and re-evaluate whether you are on the right path. There could be something new and better coming that you would miss without this opportunity to stay calm.

While on one hand, the Hanged Man asks you to welcome the pauses and reflect, on the other, the card encourages you to surrender and let go with the flow of life. You can adjust your perception or shift your energy. Moving away from the everyday running of life can just be the breath of fresh air you need, allowing you to feel more alive and for things to flow.

Reversed Hanged Man

While the Hanged Man is asking you to take a pause, you may be resisting and filling your days with more tasks that keep you busy instead, distracting you from the issue at hand. While the Universe, body, and spirit are calling for you to stop, your mind is still engaged and racing. Heed the call and create time to pause and listen.

You may be frustrated with things being on hold

by other people and circumstances. Learn to let go and accept the situation as is, even if it is against your expectations. If your life has been on hold for a while, the Reverse Hanged Man could be the sign you have been waiting for to move forward again and apply a new strategy. However, if you are content to keep waiting, especially until you feel certain of a decision, the time may never come, and this card could be the sign that you can now take a leap of faith and decide.

Death

On this card is the Messenger of Death riding a beautiful white horse and adorned in a black cloth. In his hand, he holds up a black flag with a white five-petal rose symbolizing immortality, beauty, and purification. The number five—as the number of petals—represents change. The messenger is a living skeleton, since he can move even after death. He wears a black armor that makes him invincible, so no one can destroy him. There is no preventing death—it will come. The black color he wears shows mourning and mystery. On the other hand, the horse is a sign of purity, power, and strength.

On the ground lies a royal figure that appears to be dead, while a child, bishop, and young woman plead with death to spare them. Death does not differentiate people according to class, gender, or race; he strikes anyone. There is a seemlingly mythological boat floating down the river that escorts the dead to the afterlife. The sun sets on the horizon between two towers, depicting dying each night and waking up reborn in the morning. Thus, the Death card is not just about endings, but also beginnings, change, transformations, birth, and rebirth.

Upright Death Meaning

Do not run off when you land on this card. The Death card is perhaps the most feared and misconstrued of all the tarot cards. Humans fear death—we fear the unknown and uncontrollable. Most people take the death card to literally mean dying. However, it is actually one of the most powerful and positive in the deck.

Landing on the Death card is a sign that a major phase of your life is coming to an end and a new one is about to start. The card encourages you to close the door to the past behind you, so a new door can open. You need to focus your energy on what lies ahead.

You could also be undergoing a transition, change, or transformation that calls for you to amend your ways and thinking. There is no room for the old version of yourself; they need to die so you can embrace a better version of yourself. For most people, this can be quite scary, as you do not know what to expect. The Death card could also mean that you need to get rid of any unhealthy attachments that you may have. Let them die so you can have a healthier and more fulfilling life.

Reversed Death Card

Even in reverse, the Death card talks about change—the one you are resisting. You may be concerned about embracing change since you are afraid to let go of what you are accustomed to. However, you need to realize that resisting change and being stuck in the past significantly limits your future. Admittedly, change can be unnerving for most people, but it is time to accept change. Give a new way of life a try and don't limit yourself to the past. Life moves on, and so should you. You should not live in regret; rather, take a leap of faith and move forward.

~

Temperance

Unlike the other cards that depict a figure of a certain gender, the Temperance card has an angel with wings. However, gender is not obvious, showing a balance between male and female. The angel wears a light blue robe with a square on the front and a triangle bound inside. The triangle represents humans who are bound by the Earth and the law of nature, the latter of which is symbolized by the square.

One of the angel's feet is in water, symbolizing the subconscious and need to flow with life. The other footsteps on the dry ground represent the material world and a need to be grounded. In their hands, they hold two cups, appearing to mix the waters; this action is a representative of the superconscious and subconscious minds. The water seems to be flowing between the two, indicating unity and infinity.

There is a winding path in the background that goes up a mountain range, signifying the journey that one undertakes through life. High over the mountain is a golden crown seen through a glowing light that suggests it is best to take the higher path and stay true to one's life's meaning and purpose.

Upright Temperance

The Temperance card talks about one thing: balance. Consider landing on this card as an invitation to stabilize your energy, bring patience, moderation, and balance into your life. Allow life to happen without resistance, recover your flow, and maintain order and balance in life. To achieve this, you have to be calm in all situations.

You also have to take a path that can accommodate all perspectives. Instead of being an opinionated and highly controversial person, it is best to be the peacekeeper and taking a more moderate approach. The card shows that you have a well-stipulated vision and are taking the time to do the best you can. However, you need to come up with a moderate and well-guided approach to achieve those goals. The card is also a reflection of higher learning, listening to your inner voice to guide you toward the right path.

· · ·

Reversed Temperance

When you land on the Reversed Temperance card, look closely at your life and see if you have had any excesses. You may consider the card as a warning to restore moderation and balance in your life. If you are stuck on negative habits, it is best to abstain, then slowly start balancing things out. Take time to self-evaluate and look at your priorities, then create flow in your life. By creating a balance and moderation, you reduce unnecessary stress and adjust your environment for self-healing.

The Devil

On this card is Baphomet, the Horned Goat of Mendes, who is also the Devil's most well-known satyr form. He is half goat, half-man with an inverted pentagram on his head, signifying dark magic and occultism. Originally, Baphomet stood for the balance between evil and good, human and animal, and male and female; however, over time, he started being used as a scapegoat for the things we consider as "evil" in this world."

The figure has vampire bat wings—creatures known to suck its prey's lifeblood—displaying an insight into what happens when you allow raw desire to take over. His stare hypnotizes those that go near him, and they end up under his spell and power. His right hand is raised in the Vulcan salute, while his left hand holds a lit torch.

A striking part of this card shows a naked man and woman chained to the podium where the Devil sits. The existence of the chains shows that they do not wish to be there but are captives. Interestingly, the chains around their necks are loose, thus, they can probably get out of them without much struggle. That is not all—they seem to be growing horns, becoming like the devil the more they stay and associate with him. They even have tails that depict their raw instincts and animalistic tendencies. Their tails depict fire and grapes on them, signifying lust and pleasure.

Upright Devil

You may relate to the Devil card; that is, if you are willing to be honest with yourself. The Devil card shows your darker side and the negative habits or forces that prevent you from being the best. You could be facing negative behaviors, thoughts, dependencies, habits, relationships, or addictions. You may be choosing short-term gratification but getting long-term pain. You now find yourself trapped, but it's out of your will. Simply, you are selling your soul to the Devil.

The good news is that the rope is loose on the neck, meaning that you have the control to break the negative cycle from your life. The first step to healing is an admission of the problem. By facing the problem head-on and admitting its existence, you can focus on deliberate steps to eliminating that habit, or ending that relationship. The appearance of the devil card in a reading is, in fact, an opportunity to examine those negative influences consciously and create awareness of their existence, so you can free yourself from them. You cannot deal with a problem that does not exist.

The Devil card is not all bleak—it can show strong attachments between people. Although such can be good, it is also a warning that a perfectly healthy relationship can still turn unhealthy through dependence and over-attachment. In the process, you may go over your boundaries and lose your inner guidance.

The card may be speaking about your sexuality, especially your wild side. Although it is an exciting and enriching experience to explore various sides of sexual pleasure within a sacred and safe place, it can easily turn into a danger. You, therefore, need to maintain clear boundaries of where and how you will explore your sexuality. Be cautious when choosing your partner and communicate how far you are willing to go.

Reversed Devil

Often, the Reversed Devil card can appear when you are about to experience a breakthrough. You can consider landing on this card as a call for you to achieve your highest potential, but first, you must get off the noose. Let go of any negative attachments and habits that limit your growth. You have to deal with the shadows to step into the light. You can do so by confronting your fears and anxieties and eliminating anything that is harming your inner psyche.

The card could also be a sign that you are holding a deep and dark self from those around you. You do not want anyone else to know the addictions and thoughts that you harbor. Although it can give you a good image, it also keeps you feeling guilty. By trusting someone with your secrets, you will experience a sense of relief and freedom and enjoy life better. Alternatively, you could free yourself from any unnecessary societal restrictions that hold you back and practice the principle of detachment.

The Tower

A tower is mainly associated with strength; however, the one in this card is destroyed by a lightning bolt. A strike of the lighting sets the tower ablaze and in desperation—two people jump from the windows, falling headfirst and with their arms outstretched. The scene in the tower card is of destruction and chaos.

Although the tower is a solid structure, it is built on a faulty foundation, depicting ambition that is based on false premises. The tower must, therefore, be destroyed to do away with the old ways and pave way for something new.

Upright Tower

The Tower card in a tarot reading represents a momentous and radical change. Although the card may be visually unnerving, it does not have to be frightening. All it communicates is ground-breaking change. You may be concerned that the change will only occur through a disaster—like a lightning bolt or fire—but such does not have to be so. Change is normal, and you have to be willing to embrace it, which means abandoning strongly held beliefs and perceived truths and finding other values and principles to replace them. In all this, maintain a positive attitude, knowing that you are replacing a faulty foundation with something more stable that will serve you in the long term.

Once the tower is destroyed, you will emerge stronger, resilient, and wiser with a new perspective on life. The card may also indicate spiritual awakening. You may be able to see the destruction taking action before the entire tower falls. Take this as a chance to break free from non-progressive ways of thinking and doing things that hold you back.

Reversed Tower

The Reversed Tower card suggests that you are undergoing upheave. You can feel the looming crisis and are struggling to keep it away. Although any crisis is not welcome, it could be beneficial in taking

MEANING OF TAROT CARDS—THE MAJOR ARC...   85

away your dependence on false principles. Since the foundation is weak, it should fall. Though the destruction is painful, it will result in peace. The removal of things that you are dependent on, along-side them being painful, can result in depressive feel-ings and thoughts—instead, focus your attention on being self-reliant.

The Star

On this card is a woman kneeling on the edge of a small pond while holding two water containers in both hands. From one of the containers, she pours water on the dry land to ensure it is nourished and continues with the fertility cycle. Her work is paying off; you can see the lush greenery that surrounds her.

One of her feet is on the ground, symbolizing her common sense and practical abilities, whereas the one in the water represents her intuition, listening to her inner voice, and inner resources. Her nakedness signifies purity and vulnerability. One large bright star shines behind her, signifying her core essence, while the seven small stars that surround it represent the chakras. A bird stands on a tree branch, representing the holy ibis of thought.

Upright Star

The Star card is associated with hope, strength, and renewed power to move forward with life, especially after coming right after the destruction associated with the Tower. The star reminds you of the abundance of the universe, as evidenced by the things you see. Consider this card as a reminder that you hold all you need in life within you. You only need to look inwards to find fulfillment. All you need is courage and faith that the universe will water you with blessings and you will have reasons to rejoice.

Reversed Star

Landing on the Reversed Star implies a loss of faith and hope. You may be feeling like the world is in turmoil, and challenges are no longer exciting, but overwhelming. You may also have lost hope in yourself or faith in things you believed. Thus, you lack the motivation to move forward and work toward progress. You need to evaluate where in life you are feeling hopeless and defeated. You need to nurture your sense of hope and focus on positive energy to motivate your actions with joy. By being hopeful, you can triumph over fear.

Your energy reserves could be running low. The Reversed Star asks you to take time for nourishment and self-care, spiritually and personally.

The Moon

As the name suggests, the Moon Tarot card has a full moon at night, appearing between two huge towers. The moon symbolizes dreams, intuitions, and the unconscious. With a dim light, it illuminates the path between the two towers, leading into the distance and toward higher consciousness. A dog and a wolf stand on either side of the path on the grassy field and howl at the moon, depicting our animalistic nature. One is wild and feral like the wolf, whereas the other is more civilized like a dog.

There is a small pool in the foreground that represents our watery subconscious mind. From it, a crayfish crawls, a symbol of the first steps of consciousness unfolding.

Upright Moon

The Moon card tends to appear in a tarot reading at times when you are casting your fears based on past experiences into the present and future. Painful memories can cause emotional distress now, if not addressed. If you have any negative past experiences or trauma, you need to deal with the emotions that come with them and not shove them down into your subconscious. They may prevent you from moving on with life. Such emotions make reappearances and influence you consciously and subconsciously. You, therefore, have to connect with your subconscious mind to release any anxieties or fears that hold you captive.

You can employ either therapy, hypnosis, or shamanic healing.

The Moon is not bright and illuminates only a small part of the path, an indication that you could be in a time of uncertainty without clarity. In this season, take caution in not rushing into decisions, as you cannot see the whole path. Take time to listen to your intuition and seek more information—more than what you can see. Focus on your dreams, inner guidance, and intuition to guide your judgment and decisions, as well as interpret subconscious messages.

Pay careful attention to lunar cycles and tap into their divine power. You can connect to the divine feminine and reveal visions and insights of what lies beyond today. Set your intentions on a new moon and plant seeds of opportunities. On the full moon, honor your accomplishments and set out new plans, so you can move forth with new aspects.

Reversed Moon

Landing the Reversed Moon indicates that you have had a period of dealing with fears, anxieties, and illusions, but now these destructive energies are subsiding. You are certainly in a better place now, working through your anxieties and fears and getting an understanding of their impact on your life. You are also working on ways to free yourself from their hold. You are experiencing a transformational and liberating experience.

You may believe you are not ready to address your fears and instead opt to bury them deep in your subconscious to avoid your dark side. You could also be pretending that everything is fine. Although this may work for a while, it is not sustainable in the long run. The Reverse Moon card tells you that these will resurface eventually, and it is best to deal with them once and for all.

The Reversed Moon suggests that you are receiving psychic downloads and intuitive messages, but you do not understand their meaning in your life. The message may not tally with anything you know or have read. Opt to listen to your inner voice, trust the answers from within, and tap into inner guidance to get your answers. Pay attention to your dreams, and if you can, keep a dream diary. Dreams are a way of relaying subconscious messages. If you are still not certain on what to do, look at the diary later when your mind is clear.

~

The Sun

The Sun Tarot card speaks of positivity, fulfillment, and optimism, representing the dawn after a dark night. On the card is the sun—the source of life on Earth and a symbol of life energy. Four sunflowers grow underneath a symbol of the four elements and four suits of the Minor Arcana.

In the foreground is a calm, white horse with a young, naked child sitting on it, depicting innocence, purity, and the joy of being aligned with one's inner spirit. The child's nakedness shows that he has nothing to hide. The horse is a symbol of nobility and strength.

Upright Sun

The Upright Sun card stands for abundance, success, and radiance. You will experience vitality and strength as the sun gives. You can take this card as a sign that happiness and joy are your portions. People are attracted to you because you spread joy and inspiration due to your personal fulfillment. You have a warm personality, and you bring positive energy into the lives of others. Like the sun, you are set above and in a position that enables you to share your qualities and achievements with others. Those around you experience your affection and love.

The Sun card is all about fulfillment and good feelings and shows that you possess a considerable sense of deserved confidence. The sun is shining on you and providing you with the energy to achieve your goals. Additionally, it connects you to the right powerbase that is not driven by fear or egoistical power, but rather inner and abundant energy that radiates through you. Radiate your energy throughout your world, sharing your gifts with the world. Positively use that power.

If it is a difficult time for you and challenges abide, consider the Sun card as the message you have been waiting for. Things will get better! You have the energy and zeal to work for a great future. The challenges you have faced have molded you into a better version of yourself. Abundance and success are flowing through to you. You have the confidence that everything will work out well.

As the main energy source for the world, the Sun card is energetic, reflecting a period when you can expect to have increased physical energy, general positivity, and vitality. You are full of enthusiasm, vigor, and enjoying good health.

Reversed Sun

When you land on the Reversed Sun card, it implies that you have challenges finding positive aspects to certain situations in your life. You are not feeling confident or powerful; instead, your enthusiasm and optimism are suffering. There is a cloud over your sun, blocking the light and warmth. You need not worry, as this is temporary. You need to engage your mind to remove the obstacles, and those clouds will pave way for the sun to shine.

This card calls out your inner child to play. Watch a child play and see how much joy they derive from simple things. Life can be wonderful and carefree if you can let go of many of your concerns and fears and see the goodness in it. Take time off that busy schedule, go dancing, be silly, and just play. Your heart, soul, and body will thank you.

The Reversed Sun may also mean that you are not being realistic—rather, you are overly optimistic and overconfident in some situations. You need to take into account all the important factors first before using blind optimism to keep you on the right track. Your success does not depend on optimism alone.

Judgment

So, the judgment shall come, and there is no avoiding it. The card depicts men, women, and children rising from graves with outspread arms, and looking up into the sky as a response to Angel Gabriel's trumpet call. The outstretched hands indicate that they are ready for the universe to judge them. They are going to meet the creator, have their actions weighed, and based on the results, they will spend the rest of eternity either in Heaven or Hell. In the background an extensive tidal wave and mountain range that signify that judgment is unavoidable.

Upright Judgment

The judgment card is a wake-up call for self-evaluation and the need to embrace a high level of consciousness. Your service should be for the highest good. You are having a spiritual awakening, which makes you cognizant of how you are destined for more. Do not disappoint yourself, but instead, step up, let go of old habits, and work the new version of you into the person that you should be.

This card is also an indication of the need for a life-changing decision based on both intuition and intellect. If you are unsure if the decision you are about to make is right, especially due to any long-term effects it will have, look within, be confident, and know that you are choosing the right path. Your past lessons will also guide you in making the right decision.

You may feel at ease sharing your challenges and struggles with others in a group setting. You may find someone with a similar experience who can show you a way out of trouble. Do not refuse assistance—embrace it, as it is the only way you can rise together.

Reversed Judgment

If you pick the Reverse Judgment card, it may be a sign that you have self-doubts and judge yourself harshly. The result is that you are missing opportunities and falling behind plans, and hence you feel stuck. Do not ignore your inner critic though—listen to them, acknowledge their fears, and then assure them that things will be alright. Let go of that excess caution and wear your pride and confidence as you move forward. Replace much of the criticism with positive messages to keep you going.

When reversed, the Judgment card is also an encouragement to reflect on the lessons learned so far. Without taking some time out to think clearly on matters and appreciate the lessons, it is difficult to progress forward with awareness. Forgive yourself for the past mistakes, and instead of focusing on what you would have done better, learn from them and move forward.

～

The World

On this card is a naked woman wrapped in purple cloth. She dances inside a huge laurel wreath, looking back to her past while the rest of her body moves to the front and into the future. The greenness of the wreath symbolizes success, while the red ribbon around it depicts infinity. The wreath is circular, a sign that there is a continual cycle of endings and new beginnings. Her stepping through the wreath completes a phase of her life and immediately starts another. Like the magician, she holds a wand, one in each hand, symbolizing that what the magician manifested is now completed in the world.

Similar to the wheel of fortune, the wreath has four figures—an eagle, cherub, bull, and lion—representing the zodiac signs of Scorpio, Aquarius, Taurus, and Leo. They also signify the four Tarot suits, four compass points, four evangelicals, and four elements. They guide you from one phase to the next, giving your journey balance and harmony.

Upright World

The appearance of the World in a tarot reading is indicative of a sense of achievement, fulfillment, completion, and wholeness. You have completed an aspect or period in your life successfully, bringing it to full circle, and finding this card is a sign of closure and accomplishment. You have achieved your goal, everything is working out well, you are in the right place, and you are on the right path. Because of this accomplishment, you feel complete and whole.

Having gone through the journey, it is time to reflect on the lessons you have learned and honor your achievements. Celebrate the success you earned and enjoy the satisfaction of seeing the fruits of your labor. You are now stronger, wiser, and more experienced from the triumphs and tribulations you faced during your journey. Savor the success first without running into the next big project or challenge.

If you have not yet completed the journey, do not worry; landing on this card means you are close— you may need another level of understanding to achieve your goals and enjoy success. Acknowledge how far you have come and the experience you picked along the way, and you may be surprised at how much you have achieved so far. With this reflection, you can work on the final stage of your project and bring it to a successful close. The World card symbolizes closure. You may need to tie any loose ends that may be remaining and create space for new opportunities and beginnings.

In literal terms, the World card can mean travel. You may get an opportunity to travel on a large scale or move overseas for work or study. The World card advances the principle of global awareness and universal understanding, which can be cultivated by traveling and experiencing new people and different cultures.

Reversed World

If you find the Reversed World card, it suggests that you are trying to find closure. You may be attached to a past relationship or hanging on to things from the past. You realize that to move forward and embrace the present, you need to let go of the past. Do whatever it takes to find closure, like visualization, therapy, or energy work. You have to close the cycle to start a new one.

The card could also indicate that you want to complete an important project but are unwilling to take all the steps. You may opt for the quickest or easiest paths, but you will not achieve your intended outcome by doing so. Stop running away from the tribulations that come with the entire journey—they make you stronger and give you experience. Besides, following the entire journey can contribute to a great sense of achievement once you get to the top. Enduring the challenges makes the victory sweet. You may be close to achieving your goals, but you slack off, re-energize, keep an eye on the goal and recommit to completing the project. If you are missing a piece, get creative and innovative. You must get to the finish line.

Chapter Summary

In this chapter, we looked at the tarot cards found in the Major Arcana. The Major Arcana points to major life events, carrying the weight of the message being sent home. In summary:

- There are 22 cards in the Major Arcana.
- The Major Arcana depicts a journey taken by the Fool from his naivety all through life, to the World, which represents completion and wholeness.
- Each card has a unique message that can vary depending on one's life situation at that moment and your interpretation.
- Each card has a reversed version, which offers a different meaning from the upright version, mostly showing a lack of or excess.
- The interpretations here are a guide, and not the gospel.

In the next chapter, you will learn about the meaning of the cards in the Minor Arcana, so you will be conversant with their meanings when you land on a combination of cards.

CHAPTER 4

MEANING OF TAROT CARDS—
THE MINOR ARCANA

The Minor Arcana has four suits: Cups, Swords, Wands, and Pentacles. Each of these carries its own meaning. In this section, we will look at each of the suits, as well as the meanings of each card.

The Suit of Cups

In a tarot reading, the suit of Cups is linked to emotions, creativity, the unconscious, and intuition. These cards mostly focus on relationships, connections, feelings, imagination, love, and the inner world. The suit of cups is associated with the element of water, which is thus, a frequent visual theme. Water is agile, fluid, and flowing, but it is also formative and powerful. Although it can be gentle and relaxing, it can also be forceful and powerful.

The element of water symbolizes intuition, emotions, fluidity, cleansing, and healing. Being a feminine element, it mirrors the subtle power that women have. Water is adaptable, receptive, purifying, and flowing. Hearts in playing cards correspond to Cups in a tarot deck.

. . .

Meaning of Cups

Drawing cups in a tarot reading means you are using your heart to think rather than your head, explaining your habitual reactions and spontaneous responses to situations. Cups tend to be associated with fantasy, romanticism, creativity, and imagination.

On the flip side, cups may indicate being dispassionate, disengaged, fantasizing, and having unrealistic expectations. On the other hand, it could be indicating repressed emotions, lack of creativity, and an inability to express oneself.

Ace of Cups

On the Ace of Cups is a chalice overflowing with sparkling water, symbolizing a pristine and pure emotion. The cup is a representation of the vessel of the subconscious mind, while the five streams flowing from it depict the five senses, intuition, and emotion flowing from within. You must listen to the inner voice, and no matter the situation, remain true to it, for you to have overflowing happiness and joy.

The cup is held by hands that seem to be sliding from the cloud, a sign of being aware of spiritual energy and power. The hand seems to be offering a drink to the querent, offering spiritual and emotional fulfillment. Lotus blossoms are covering the area below the hand, a symbol of the human spirit's awakening. The cards speak of divinity with a dove descending toward the overflowing cup, depicting the flow of divine love through the subconscious to the conscious.

The Ace of Cups shows that it is time to lose emotional baggage and live life to the fullest. You have a chance to have a new beginning and may only come when you open yourself to the possibility of starting new relationships, which can be emotionally fulfilling. Depending on your current situation, the release may be emotional or spiritual. If you have been alone or deeply hurt for a long time, getting the Ace of Cups is an indication of a fresh start. By opening yourself up to new beginnings and opportunities, it becomes easier to let go of the past and enjoy love, relationships, and spiritual learnings. The Ace of Cups offers you a chance to have some joy and happiness, so drink up!

When overturned or in reverse, water in the overflowing cup then pours out and becomes empty, wasting the gift of water. You may have been enduring the pain of emotional instability for some time and are deprived of joy—it flowed out. If you are an artist or in the creative department, this card could indicate a creative block; the waters are no longer flowing. Whatever the situation, getting this card calls for you to examine *why* the water is flowing out. Who holds control of the cup and is allowing it to overturn? Find ways to put the cup back up.

Two of Cups

Like the Ace of Cups, the Two of Cups card represents the flow of love, not from within, but between two people. On the card are a man and a woman swapping cups. A symbol of Hermes' caduceus on the card relates to trade, a cosmic energy, negotiation, protection, duality, and proper conduct. There is a chimera above the caduceus, which is a symbol of the passion and fire that govern the partnership.

The Two of Cups card depicts positivity and suggests the creation of partnerships and deep connections that are based on compassion, shared value, and unconditional love. Your emotions are intertwined, and your feelings affect each other profoundly. You are both focused on creating a mutually-beneficial relationship, since each of you sees the potential the other person brings on board. The card represents mutual respect, commitment, love, and a balanced relationship.

In reverse, the Two of Cups card suggests that there is a lack of balance that was once there. Since the balance is an integral part of the relationship, its breaking can lead to discord and disconnect. Instead of the attraction that there once was, now there is repelling. Small things that were non-issues are now becoming problems, signaling to the existence of resentment. There is a communication breakdown that only makes imbalance and resentment worse. You need to be the bigger person and open up about the situation. You may realize the balance is easier to restore than you previously thought; however, the restoration can only happen if you have self-love. You must love, respect, and honor the authentic version of you. When you have accepted yourself and your faults, you can cultivate meaningful relationships with others.

Three of Cups

The Three of Cups card has three women holding their cups up in the air in what seems to be a celebration. The card suggests good times, which is emphasized by the wreaths that the women wear in their hair. Wreaths signify happiness and are usually worn when there is success or victory. The field of flowers and fruits that the women are in adds to the joy emanating from this card. You can feel the beauty, happiness, compassion, and growth that the women in the card project. The three women symbolize your important circle of friends, family, or the people you turn to and call for support.

As seen on the card, it depicts a period of happiness where you can spend time with people who matter to you, have fun, and celebrate. During this time, you can forget the worries of your everyday life. Finding this card can mean a happy reunion with someone whom you have not met in a long time or a celebration for you or someone close to you. Prepare to spend quality and celebratory time with the people you love.

If your social life has been challenging, you can take landing on this card as a sign that the period of problems is over. You will solve those problems and get back your circle of friends. A great reunion and reconnection await.

The Reversed Three of Cups can mean that you are too busy and do not find time to socialize with friends and family. You are probably losing touch with friends and growing apart from each other. You must, therefore, put in effort to ensure that your friendship is not neglected.

On the other hand, it could suggest a lack of harmony and balance within your social circle. You may be feeling isolated because of certain negatives, such as scandals, gossip, and envy.

Four of Cups

Here, a young man sits under a tree on the top of a mountain, his arms crossed and in deep in meditation and contemplation. So engrossed is he in his thoughts that he is not even aware of the outstretched arm that offers him a cup. On his feet are an additional three cups that he is also not aware of or concerned about.

The four cups symbolize our inclination to take the things we have for granted and appreciate the treasures that the universe gives us. Although the answers are lying right at our feet most often, we opt to focus on the things we do not have. Opportunities then pass us by as we contemplate.

You may land on the Four of Cups when you are feeling stuck, discouraged, bored, or dissatisfied. You may feel like you lost your passion and happiness. The Four of Cups is a call to self-evaluate your attitude and open your eyes. The answers you seek may be lying right before you and the hand is offering a solution, but your mental stubbornness may not be allowing you to move forward.

An appearance of this card could also indicate that you have numerous opportunities and new invitations flowing toward you, but you are turning them down. They may be of no interest to you or your plate is full. Use your wisdom to prioritize and decide what is important and pick that which aligns with your future. You can let the others pass along. On the other hand, it is also an indication to turn your energy and attention internally and realign to a new phase in life. During this time, you may decline opportunities that come to you, but know that you are working on yourself to accept those that are a better fit for you. For you, this is a preparatory phase for the next big project.

A notable aspect about the Four of Cups is that, although the young man does not accept the cups, he also does not reject them. You may believe that you are not ready for some tasks or opportunities. You may also be waiting for more information or a sign before taking up a role. Take your time and accept when you are ready to embark on for your next journey.

In reverse, the Four of Cups may signal that you are eager to start a new chapter. You are now more aware of what is around you and willing to embrace new ideas, people, and places. You are choosing to appreciate what you have and make the best out of it. Take that opportunity you desire, go on an adventure, and discover what life has to offer.

Five of Cups

The card shows a figure clad in a black cloak and hiding his face in despair. Your emotions dip from looking at this card as it talks of pain and loss. Five cups are on the ground with three of them having fallen while the others are standing. The figure, however, only seems to be focused on mourning the fallen cups and does not notice the standing ones. A powerful river flows between him and a house appearing in the distance, an indication of a powerful emotion separating him from home.

The card is a symbol of disappointment and how bad you feel when things do not go as expected. Although it can be disheartening to be in such a situation, you are dwelling on the past and spilled milk instead of moving to another positive perspective. You are in regret and wallowing in self-pity instead of moving forward. The spilled water shows a missed opportunity that you are incapable of letting go of. The problem is, however, more emotional than it is financial or material. You need to address your emotions. By being so caught up in past disappointments, you are likely missing out on the joys that the future holds.

When it is reversed, the Five of Cups card symbolizes significant progress, recovery from regrets, and acceptance of the past. You are realizing the consequences of your actions and appreciating the lessons learned, and you are ready to move ahead. You may recognize that the painful experience built your character by equipping you with strength and resilience. You can now accomplish more, are ready to focus on the two remaining cups, and can make the best out of life.

Six of Cups
The card has six cups with white flowers. In the

foreground is a boy who leans down to pass a cup to a girl who looks up to him with love and respect. The children symbolize childhood memories. The act of passing flowers indicates the passing of traditions and happy reunions. The card speaks of harmony, cooperation, and love.

The children seem to be in a large home or castle, depicting safety, security, and comfort. An older man is walking away in the distance, suggesting that there is no need to dwell on adult issues. You should enjoy being young and free.

Everything about this card stands for happiness, innocence, generosity, and childhood. You may want to go back to happier times when you were young. You could be looking for that aspect in you that vanished and believe that looking to the past is the only way to regain it and be happy. However, be careful not to live in the past. The card could also mean that you will be returning to a former or familiar place for a reunion with people. There is comfort in being back home with people who genuinely love you.

You may be hanging on to the past, and although it is comforting, you have to let go eventually and make your own life. You can use the past happy memories to guide your path to a fulfilling present and future.

You could be experiencing a disconnect from your childhood dreams. Although the failure to achieve those dreams can be painful, do a reality check and embrace the present, setting realistic goals and working towards them.

Seven of Cups

A person stands facing away and contemplates seven cups floating on clouds filled with various gifts from jewels and wreaths, while others contain snakes and dragons. The cups and clouds depict the man's dreams and wishes and their content is a lesson to be careful about what you ask or wish for.

Drawing this card in a reading implies the need to see the visions in your imagination clearly in the real world. You have to be careful with your wishes and alert to your choices. Although having dreams can be good and exciting, taking action to achieve your dreams is certainly a better choice. You may be guided by illusions floating in the clouds. You have to identify what is real and focus on that.

The card could mean you are undecided about the many options. Take time to weigh the pros and cons before making a choice.

Similar to the upright card, the reversed card indicates that your focus is on fantasy with no grounding in reality. You are, thus, unclear about what you seek. You may be unwilling to face reality and opt to escape it through fantasy and imagination.

On the other hand, this card could mean an end to illusion and acceptance of reality.

Eight of Cups

The cloaked figure on this card seems to be turned, leaving the eight golden cups behind and going to the barren land. The arrangement of the cups makes it look like one is missing, which symbolizes a lack of emotional fulfillment and wholeness. The nearby river signifies his emotions, while the mountains speak of a tough journey ahead. The moon illuminates his sky, suggesting that he is leaving at night, or rather, escaping.

The card may be an indication of transition or change. You may have to leave a disappointing situation, despite having invested in it heavily. If you are not getting returns or it is disappointing, leave it all behind and move forward.

You may be lacking emotional or spiritual fulfillment and are dissatisfied with life. Instead of sitting around hoping for change, it may be time to move on and seek fulfillment. Letting go may be difficult, but it will enable you to find true happiness elsewhere. You could opt to take a spiritual journey.

On the other hand, it could mean that you are trying to escape a problem and aren't dealing with psychological issues and concerns. Instead, you repress your feelings and pretend it's okay. You have to figure out what brings you happiness, peace, and contentment and pursue that.

The Reversed Eight of Cups indicates confusion on which path to take, since you lack awareness of what is good for you. You may not have clear goals and are always going wherever life takes you. Have the courage to go for a change that will make your life better. The card could also mean you are aware that you need to make a change, but you are afraid and keep doing the same thing instead. You want to change but are afraid of losing the comfort you are used to.

Nine of Cups

This card shows a man sitting comfortably on a wooden bench with crossed arms and a smiling face, which speaks of satisfaction and contentment. He has on a red headdress, which is a symbol of an active mind. Nine golden cups are well-arranged in the background, a representation of both spiritual and material success and fulfillment.

Everything about this card shouts self-satisfaction, as the emotional journey of the cups nears a close. Having endured the challenges in trying to find joy and purpose after a loss, received gifts from the world, and left comforts in search of greater heights, it is time to celebrate your achievements. Being the wish card, this card suggests that your desires and perfect dream are about to happen, leading to extreme satisfaction and happiness.

A positive card even in reverse, the Nine of Cups asks you to consider what you want in life more seriously. You are looking for genuine fulfillment; however, the card could also mean that despite achieving your purpose and being celebrated by others, you still feel like there is a missing piece. Your desires may be more and appear never-ending, or you feel inadequate. You need to address the cause of your lack of confidence.

The card may also indicate that you are placing value on your blessings rather than your quality of life. Your relationships are the real treasures, so guard and appreciate them.

Ten of Cups

On this card is a couple in a loving embrace in a green garden and facing a beautiful house. There are two children playing joyously too. The couple's relationship is stable, and they enjoy the blessing of abundance, as depicted by beautiful children and a comfortable home. The land is green, signifying fertility, and the presence of a river shows the flow of the couple's feelings and peace. There are ten cups in the sky in an arc, a symbol of blessings from Heaven, while the rainbow indicates that sorrows and end times are ending. The family can now enjoy a happy life.

Getting this card could indicate "having it all," since it embodies joy, happiness, emotional satisfaction, and contentment in your relationship, companion, or family. At this point, your needs, wants, and desires have been fulfilled, so you are satisfied and filled with harmony, peace, love, and comfort. Be thankful for the blessings.

This card also indicates a true, emotional fulfillment where success is shared, creating a sense of family and community. You can now live happily ever after with your family.

Unlike the unity in the upright card, in the reversed card, the strong bonds are twisted or broken. You may find that you are growing apart from your family and community. You may also realize that the hope for happy times is dwindling with nothing to show. You can only have harmony by treating each other well.

Page of Cups

Here, a young woman is at the seashore, wearing a blue floral-printed tunic and holding a golden cup. She also wears a beret and a long scarf. A fish pops out of the cup, so she can neither drink nor toast, as the fish is staring at her. The unexpected entrance of the fish shows creative inspiration that appears from the blues when you are open to receive it.

The Page of Cups suggests the need to stay open to new ideas, even when you least expect them, and particularly those that stem from intuitive inspiration. You may also be facing a difficult situation and are no longer chasing your dreams; it is time to approach things from a different view. Pay attention to your intuition and persist with the belief that everything is possible.

In reverse, this card may point to a block in creativity or lack of inspiration. You could also be doing some projects, not for the joy and satisfaction that you would get, but for other things, like money. Remember how much joy you derived from your work and reclaim your creativity.

Knight of Cups

A young knight rides on a white horse while holding a cup like a messenger. He moves slowly in peace and calmness. The horse symbolizes energy, drive, and power, while its white color speaks of light, purity, and spirituality.

Although this knight appears feminine, he remains worthy. He has a better touch with his intuition and emotions, hence his charm and attraction. Landing on this card is a message of a person or event with an emotional benefit. You may also engage in a project that gives you creative and emotional value.

Unlike the sober and calm knight, the reversed Knight of Cups indicates that you are allowing emotions to carry you toward a dangerous point of inability to take action. You may be jumping to conclusions without bothering to learn the necessary information. The card could also depict the initial appeal of something that ends up being disappointing.

Queen of Cups

The beautiful queen has her throne on the ocean's edge and holds a closed golden cup with handles that look like angels. The cup being closed indicates that her feelings and thoughts stem from the subconscious mind and deep within her soul. There are images of fish, sea-nymphs, and scallop shells that decorate her stone throne, symbolizing the unconscious mind. The water depicts spirit, perception, and emotion. Her feet rest on colorful pebbles but do not touch the water, showing that although she is connected to her emotions, they don't overwhelm her.

She is nurturing, compassionate, sensitive, and caring. You are embodying energy by being nurturing, supporting others, caring deeply, and being compassionate. Although you are emphatic and let others express themselves, you are grounded enough not to take on their emotional issues. However, it may be time to also take help from others.

You are intuitive, in the flow, and creative. You have a trusted inner voice but should take the time to tend to your emotional health before helping others. Self-love is important, as it breeds compassion.

In reverse, the Queen of Cups implies that you are not in tune with your emotions and may be unable to express your feelings clearly. You end up bottling your emotions and may be feeling stressed. On the other hand, it could mean that your mind is wandering and your imagination is running away. Before giving your emotions control, try to figure out if they are trustworthy. Ask yourself if those dreams can be turned into reality and aim for emotional stability.

King of Cups

A king with a fish-shaped amulet sits on a throne. The fish is a symbol of his spirit and creativity, which thrives in the calm waters around him. Behind him, a fish jumps out of the water on the right side, and on the other side, a ship appears, symbolizing the emotional and material worlds. The card talks of balance.

As an influential card, the King of Cups stands for emotion, creativity, and the unconscious. The king calls for a balance between emotions and intellect and calls you to build a strong relationship between your feelings and understanding. You can enhance harmony among the people because you can be both diplomatic and political. In essence, balance your emotions and control them.

In reverse, this king is moody, volatile, and emotionally manipulative. You may be unable to balance the needs of those who look up to you; being cold to some, warm to others, or manipulative. Although it may not be you, there could be someone who is usually emotionally unstalbe, but who is now becoming vengeful, vindictive, and manipulative.

The Suit of Swords

The Swords focus on the mind and intellect. They represent logic, intelligence, change, power, ambition, force, truth, courage, oppression, communication, and conflict and are linked to the element of air. The focus of these cards is on the power of the intellect that can be double-edged like the sword. On the flip side, the swords can be harsh, abusive, angry, guilty, judgmental, and lack empathy. Swords correspond to spades.

Ace of Swords

This card depicts a glowing hand holding a sword appearing from a cloud, symbolizing mind, intellect, and the divine.

This card symbolizes a wave of new intellectual energy. You could be on the edge of a breakthrough or success. You have mental clarity and a sharp mind.

In reverse, the Ace of Swords depicts chaos, re-thinking of ideas, confusion, clouded judgment, and brutality.

Two of Swords

A blindfolded woman sits holding onto a sword in each hand. Rocks and crags surround the sea in her background, obstructing ships and vessels, signi-fying stalling. The blindfold presents a situation where she cannot see either the problem nor the solu-tion clearly. The two swords may depict a stalemate or two different directions. The moon on the right side may bring out the role of deception and illusion in times of dilemmas.

The appearance of this card signifies a stalemate, being stuck in the middle, denial, difficult choices, and potentially some hidden information. You must weigh the pros and cons of each choice, then apply your head and heart to find the path that aligns with your higher self.

In reverse, this card stands for confusion, indeci-sion, anxiety, information overload, hesitancy, and stalemate.

. . .

Three of Swords

On this card is a floating heart pierced by three swords. There are heavy clouds above it and a heavy downpour in the background.

Landing on this card signifies betrayal, heartbreak, hurt, sorrow, loss, trauma, grief, rejection, and discouragement. The mind serves us well during such times, so think logically and prepare to determine how to minimize the pain.

In reverse, it depicts recovery, forgiveness, healing, repressing emotions, and reconciliation.

Four of Swords

The calm and stillness that comes with this card is a relief from the pain of the three swords. There is a carving of a knight lying upon a tomb in a church, with three swords hanging above him and a fourth lying beneath him. While the three swords signify the suffering, the fourth shows that it is over. Behind the statue are a woman and a child giving a sense of warmth. The knight's hands are in a praying position.

The card depicts retreat, a moment of rest, relaxation, self-protection, peace, sanctuary, rejuvenation, and recuperation after the chaos.

In reverse, this card can signify restlessness, burnout, stagnation, deep contemplation, and exhaustion.

. . .

Five of Swords

A sly young man looks at the people he has conquered and has five swords won from them. Two of the people walk away with a slouch, indicating loss, sadness, and defeat. The sky above is cloudy and tumultuous, showing that all is not well.

Pulling this card can indicate that you are in a conflict, argument, or dispute. You may also be facing hostility, stress, intimidation, bullying, or aggression.

If you pull a reverse card of this, it may point at a resolution, compromise, revenge, reconciliation, regret, and cutting losses.

Six of Swords

On this card, a woman and a child are in a boat being rowed toward land. They seem to be leaving something behind, considering how the woman's head is covered.

Like the woman leaving, landing on this card may mean departure, accepting lessons, distance, leaving something behind, and moving on.

In reverse, you may be stuck in the past, trapped, running away from problems, or returning to trouble.

. . .

Seven of Swords

Here, a man runs away sneakily from a sort of a camp, carrying five swords with him and leaving two others on the ground. Although he seems confident to have made away, a group of soldiers still see and pursue him.

The main focus of this card is deception and betrayal. It points at scheming, lies, trickery, strategy, sneakiness, cunning, and resourcefulness.

In reverse, it may signify regret, maliciousness, confession, conscience, self-deceit, and imposter syndrome.

Eight of Swords

The Eight of Swords card has a bound and blindfolded woman surrounded by eight swords and seemingly trapped. The scenario depicts limiting beliefs, mindsets, and thoughts. There is water pooled at her feet, which suggests her intuition may help her see what she cannot.

You may feel restricted and trapped by certain circumstances. You may have a victim mentality, self-imposed restriction, or negative thoughts.

When reversed, it could indicate self-acceptance, freedom, and embracing a new perspective.

Nine of Swords

A woman sits on her bed holding her head in her hands. She appears as if she awoke from a bad nightmare and is upset, fearful, and anxious. Hanging on her wall are nine swords, while a carving of a defeated person is on her bed. Her quilt has roses and other astrological symbols. She appears to be the woman from Eight of Swords card having escaped, but she is still haunted by the experience.

Like the woman, you are likely fearful, anxious, negative, and in despair. You may have escaped a nasty experience, but you are at a breaking point, isolated, and faced with nightmares.

On the flip side, the card may suggest a recovery, reaching out, shame, guilt, learning to cope, hope, facing life, or a mental health issue.

Ten of Swords

A man lies face-down on the ground, covered from his chest to his legs with a red cloth. He has been stabbed in the back with ten swords, an attack which he clearly did not see coming. The air is still with black and a cloudy sky, symbols of the negativity and fear that come with death. The still waters add a sense of finality. On the horizon, the sun seems to be rising.

The card points to a low point in life, ruin,

collapse, exhaustion, failure, bitterness, dead-end, betrayal, and victimization.

In reverse, it signifies healing, lessons learned, improvement, relapse, and survival.

Page of Swords

Here, a youth stands on a rocky precipice with turbulent clouds, wind-blown trees, and tossed hair. She has a sword in her hand and seems determined and energetic with a touch of defiance, ready to pounce.

This card symbolizes mental agility, alertness, vigilance, communication, wit, inspiration, and curiosity.

However, on the flip side, it indicates that you may be insulting, rude, a poor planner, sarcastic, cynical, and scatter-brained.

Knight of Swords

An armor-clad knight on a powerful white horse charges ahead with his sword held high, symbolizing his dedication to his mission. Storm clouds form in the background, and the tree bends in strong winds, yet he still heads directly into it.

As seen with the knight, landing on this card may mean that you are ambitious, fast-thinking, action-oriented, and driven to succeed.

In reverse, it suggests that you may be restless, impulsive, burned out, and unfocused.

Queen of Swords

She sits high on her cherub-decorated throne with a stern face and looking into the distance. She faces the future while lifting her left hand and holds a sword straight and high in her right, a sign that she looks for the truth in all matters. In the background, clouds gather and a strong wind blows, signifying change.

This card may mean that you are independent and perceptive and have clear boundaries, unbiased judgment, and direct communication.

In reverse, it indicates that you are overly emotional, cold-hearted, cruel, and easily influenced.

King of Swords

The king sits on his throne holding an upward-facing, double-edged sword in his right hand. He wears a blue tunic, symbolizing spiritual understanding, while the butterflies on the throne's back indicate transformation.

An appearance of this card indicates mental clarity, authority, truth, and intellectual power.

In reverse, the King of Swords suggests quiet

power, manipulation, irrationality, abuse of power, and dishonesty.

Suit of Wands

The suit of Wands is associated with the element of fire and represents inspiration, passion, and willpower. Since the cards imbue energy, they also tend to come along with the action, lack of direction, and recklessness.

Ace of Wands

A hand sticks out of a cloud holding a wand. The hand is offering the wand with leaves sprouting, representing spiritual and material balance. A castle appears in the distance, a sign of future opportunities.

In an upright position, this card represents creativity, inspiration, new passion, initiative, energy, and enthusiasm. It is one of the boldest cards found in this suit, telling you just to go for it.

In reverse, it signifies a lack of passion, low energy, blocks, delays, and hesitancy.

Two of Wands

A man stands on some kind of castle, holding a

miniature globe in his right hand that shows potential for his life's expansion and more experiences. He looks down on the large terrain, with the ocean on his left side and land on the right. He wears an orange tunic—a symbol for enthusiasm—and a red hat, signifying a hunger for adventure.

The card speaks of progress, including planning, risk-taking, moving forward, decision-making, first steps, and leaving comfort. The card also depicts discovery and encourages you to strive forward.

In reverse, this card signifies risk avoidance, poor planning, over-analysis, not taking action, and playing it safe.

Three of Wands

A man stands on the edge of a cliff, overlooking the mountain and the ocean. From his position, he sees everything that lies ahead. There are wands planted on the ground, and he holds one in his hands. He appears to reflect on his plans and how to make them successful.

The upright Three of Wands signifies momentum, growth, expansion, confidence, foresight, overseas opportunities, and looking ahead.

In reverse, it means delays, lack of progress, frustration, lack of foresight, playing small, and limitations.

. . .

Four of Wands

Here, a couple is dancing beneath a welcome wreath tied between four crystal-tipped wands. The card has a canopy of flowers, similar to that of traditional Jewish ceremonies. There appears to be a welcome party for the couple.

In its upright position, the card denotes home, celebrations, reunions, parties, belonging, community, and celebrations.

In reverse, it depicts a lack of support, home conflict, feeling unwelcome, instability, and a lack of roots.

Five of Wands

Five men hold and brandish their wands up in the air, displaying a disagreement of a sorts. However, the men are relaxed as they brandish the swords, showing that the argument is not fierce.

The upright card depicts arguments, rivals, competition, rivalry, conflict, tension, and clashes of ego.

In reverse, it shows the end of conflicts, truces, peace, harmony, cooperation, and avoiding conflicts.

Six of Wands

A man wears a wreath of victory proudly around

his head and rides a white horse through a cheering crowd.

The card means victory, success, rewards, recognition, pride, praise, and acclaim.

In reverse, it indicates failure, lack of achievement, lack of recognition, and no rewards.

Seven of Wands

On this card, a man stands on a tall hill with opponents challenging him from below. He appears to be defending his position and retaliating with an attack. His shoes do not match, symbolizing uneven ground or instability in life.

This card stands for protectiveness, defending one's rights and territories, and standing up for oneself.

In reverse, it shows you are giving up, yielding, surrendering, admitting defeat, and have a lack of self-belief.

Eight of Wands

Eight staves—or what appears to be blossomed wands—seem to be suspended in the air or traveling at full speed. The background is a clear sky with a beautiful landscape and a river streaming. The wands seem to be about to land, indicating the end of a long journey.

Drawing an upright card displays speed, movement, quick decision, sudden changes, excitement, and progress.

Picking out a reverse of this card depicts delays, waiting, hastiness, unpreparedness, slowness, and losing momentum.

Nine of Wands

A weary-looking man holds a wand with eight others standing behind him; he looks injured, yet ready for the next battle and geared to win. On this card is a mix of triumph, hope, and challenges.

The upright of this card shows perseverance, resilience, fatigue, closeness to success, grit, and last stand.

In reverse, it shows rigidity, stubbornness, defensiveness, giving up, and a refusal to compromise.

Ten of Wands

On this card, a man carries a heavy burden of wood and ten bundled wands, approaching a nearby town. He looks tired and bends under the weight, but the struggle is almost over. He is almost at the final destination, so he soldiers on.

The upright Ten of Wands displays burden, responsibility, obligation, struggle, stress, completion, hard work, and burning out.

In reverse, this card depicts carrying a burden, doing it all, failure to delegate, collapsing, feeling overburdened, having too much responsibility, and breakdowns.

Page of Wands

A well-dressed young man holds a long staff boldly while standing on barren land and looking interestedly at some green leaves growing from the top. The salamanders on his shirt symbolize transformation from bad to good. He stands still with his staff on the ground, showing that he is yet to take action, despite being inspired by the sprouting staff. Although the land is barren, he has the potential to find better fortunes.

The upright form of this card indicates inspiration, discovery, limitless, fresh ideas, free spirit, potential, and ideas.

In reverse, it may mean redirection of energy, self-limiting beliefs, lack of ideas, laziness, hastiness, impatience, unreliability, distraction, and boredom.

Knight of Wands

He sits on his orange horse in full armor and ready for action. He wears a yellow shirt with decorations of salamanders, and his helmet has red plumes. In his hand is a large wand, and he is determined to be successful. He is fiery, from the salamanders on his shirt to the flame-colored horse mane.

The upright Page of Wands may indicate courage, charm, heroism, a hot temper, free spirit, energy, and rebellion.

When reversed, the card may mean arrogance, passiveness, dominance, a lack of self-control, volatility, recklessness, and impatience.

Queen of Wands

The queen sits majestically on the throne, facing a sign of fire and strength. In her left hand is a sunflower, and there are images of sunflowers carved into the throne, an indication of fertility, happiness, and satisfaction. In her right hand is her wand, which is beginning to bloom—a symbol of life. There is a black cat at her feet, which may show occultism and witchcraft, while also being an indication of deep intuition.

Landing on the upright queen of wands may mean that you are confident, passionate, self-assured, vivacious, optimistic, charismatic, determined, and social.

In reverse, it may indicate that you are being demanding, jealous, selfish, vengeful, temperamental, and have low confidence.

. . .

King of Wands

The king has a blossoming wand in his hand, representing his creativity and passion for life. The salamander and lion decorate his throne and cape—a sign of fire and strength. The salamander that bites its tail depicts infinity and a drive to overcome obstacles.

When you pick the King of Wants, you may be showing qualities of leadership, an ability to take control, boldness, daring decisions, and have a great vision and optimism.

When in reverse, it may mean that you are forceful, tyrannical, domineering, a weak leader, powerless, and vicious.

∾

Suit of Pentacles

The suit of Pentacles is associated with worldly and material things, including security, health, nature, stability, and prosperity. In a reading, they point to aspects such as career, household, business investments, long-term future, and your sensuality. On the negative side, the pentacles appear as possessiveness, jealousy, greed, misery, and unbridled ambition.

Pentacles belong to the earth element and correspond to Diamonds in playing cards.

Ace of Pentacles

On this card, a single mysterious hand appears from the clouds, holding something like a gold coin, and its surface is engraved with a pentagram. There is a garden below the hand with flowers and other vegetation flourishing, indicating growth, fertility, and prosperity. There is also a mountain on the card that represents the necessary ambition required to drive our search for the pentacles. The presence of a flowing creek indicates the flow of our emotions toward ambition.

In an upright position, the Ace of Pentacles displays prosperity, new venture, and opportunity.

If you land on the reverse form, it may indicate a missed chance or lost opportunities.

Two of Pentacles

A man dances and juggles two large coins here. The pentacles have the infinite sign, showing that he can manage all issues that come his way with grace. Two ships ride the giant waves in the background, a symbol of the balance the man needs. Despite the chaos, he dances with joy.

The upright form of this card may mean that you are adapting to change and balancing decisions and priorities.

In the reverse, it may depict a loss of balance, disorganization, and being overwhelmed.

Three of Pentacles

On this card is a young cathedral apprentice with

two people—a priest and a nobleman, holding a piece of parchment with cathedral plans. As the apprentice explains the progress, the others listen, so they can offer guidance.

Pulling out this card may signify that you are enjoying collaboration, teamwork, and building.

When the reversed form of this card appears, it may symbolize disorganization, group conflict, and a lack of teamwork.

Four of Pentacles

Here, a man sits on a stool, balancing a pentacle on his head. He clutches another between his hands tightly, while the other two are secured under his feet. It is apparent that he is not allowing anyone to get his pentacles, but on the other hand, he cannot move due to how tightly he protects them.

The upright of this card may mean you are being possessive, stingy, a hoarder, insecure, or guarded. The card can also point at stability, savings, security, wealth, materialism, frugality, and boundaries.

In reverse, it shows generosity, giving, openness, reckless spending, and financial insecurity.

Five of Pentacles

By now, you may have noted the fives in the tarot suits symbolize adversity. In this suit, two people walk outside while it snows. They appear to lack life's necessities. One of them has crutches, while the other covers her head with a shawl, walking barefoot in the snow. A glass stained with five pentacles can be seen on the black wall in the background, probably a church.

The upright of this card indicates isolation, hardship, adversity, alienation, struggle, disgrace, loss, and feelings of abandonment.

When reversed, this card may mean recovery from loss, acceptance, forgiveness, overcoming adversity, and positive changes.

Six of Pentacles

A man dresses in a purple robe here, which is a symbol of wealth and status. On one hand is a balanced scale, displaying fairness and equality. His other hand gives money to beggars kneeling at his feet.

If you pull out this card, it may suggest generosity, sharing, gratitude, material help, support, and a sense of community.

If you pull the card in its reverse, it suggests inequality, power dynamics, gifts with strings attached, abuse of generosity, or extortion.

Seven of Pentacles

A man rests on his shovel, admiring the fruits and blossoms in the garden. Although he seems fatigued by how he lays his head over his hands, he admires the seven pentacles in the lush vegetation. His hard work has paid off, but he does not harvest yet—a sign that he is focused on his long-term goals.

The upright of this card may mean it is the time for rewards, harvest, progress, growth, and results. It also relates to effort and investment, including the planning, patience, and perseverance necessary to have a good harvest.

In reverse, it signifies unfinished work, impatience, setbacks, little effort, procrastination, and a lack of rewards.

Eight of Pentacles

A young man focuses on etching eight gold coins with a pentacle shape. The town appears to be far into the background, showing that he is isolated and concentrating on his work.

The upright Eight of Pentacles symbolizes craftsmanship, talent, skill, expertise, commitment, dedication, and accomplishment.

On its reverse side, it displays a lack of motivation and drive, poor skills, low quality, laziness, mediocrity, or a dead-end job.

. . .

Nine of Pentacles

A woman stands within a vineyard, wearing a long dress adorned with sunflowers while a falcon sits peacefully on her hand. The vines are full of grapes and golden coins, displaying success and a plentiful harvest. In the background is a castle, indicating wealth.

The card shows success, self-sufficiency, rewarded effort, achievement, and material security.

In the reverse, it depicts being guarded, material instability, living beyond one's means, and superficiality.

Ten of Pentacles

An old man sits in an archway leading into a large estate surrounded by younger people and dogs. His robe has moon crescents and grapevines for decorations, which are symbols of matter and spirit joining together. Alongside the happy couple with him is a child playing with a dog.

The Ten of Pentacles is synonymous with satisfaction and permanence. Landing on it signifies family, ancestry, legacy, roots, inheritance, affluence, tradition, stability, and foundations.

In reverse, it may indicate family disputes, debt, bankruptcy, instability, fleeting success, and breaking of traditions.

. . .

Page of Pentacles

A young man stands alone in a field surrounded by flowers with a furrowed field and lush trees in the background. He holds a coin in his hand that takes all his attention, rendering him unaware of his surroundings. The coin represents security, ambition, wealth, and sensuality.

The Page of Pentacles represents one as grounded, diligent, and loyal. It may also mean you are ambitious, faithful, goal-oriented, consistent, a good planner, diligent, and dependable.

In reverse, it indicates that you may be immature, foolish, lazy, irresponsible, a procrastinator, and an underachiever. It could also mean poor prospects and missed opportunities.

Knight of Pentacles

The knight is in a field atop a dark horse, preparing for the next harvest. He holds a gold coin in his hand and carefully considers it. Unlike other adventurous knights, this one has realized he can be more successful in a field.

The Knight of Pentacles is displayed as practical, efficient, reliable, stoic, committed, patient, and hard-working.

In reverse, he can be dull, a workaholic, irresponsible, lazy, and lack initiative.

. . .

Queen of Pentacles

She holds a golden coin and sits on a decorated throne surrounded by beautiful floral gardens and blossoming trees. Various beasts decorate the Earth, a symbol of nature and abundance. There is a pouncing rabbit on the bottom right side of the card, symbolizing fertility, high energy, and caution in watching where one leaps.

The Queen of Pentacles shows that you may be nurturing, generous, caring, practical, sensible, and welcoming, or have a good business sense.

On the reverse side, she may depict selfishness, jealousy, greediness, intolerance, envy, self-absorption, and materialism.

King of Pentacles

The king is regal and sophisticated. His throne, on which he sits, is adorned with bull carvings and vines, and his robe is decorated with images of grapevines. Around him are different kinds of plants, flowers, and vines displaying his material success. His right-hand holds a scepter while his left has a pentacle-engraved coin. In the background is a castle —a sign of effort and determination.

The King of Pentacles is associated with prosperity, security, abundance, patriarchy, reliability, ambition, protectiveness, provision, and business acumen.

In reverse, this king can be greedy, materialistic,

exploitative, possessive, chauvinistic, wasteful, and make poor financial decisions.

Chapter Summary

In this chapter, we looked at the cards in the four suits found in Minor Arcana. We learned that:

- Each card can have different meanings, depending on your intuition and the deck you are using.
- You should familiarise yourself with the different cards.
- As you read the cards, let them talk to you —what you perceive may be different from what someone else will.

In the next chapter, you will learn about the different tarot spreads that are ideal for use as a beginner.

CHAPTER 5
TAROT SPREADS

Although reading tarot is an intuitive practice, you need to design your procedure well. Tarot spreads denote the pattern of cards picked during a reading. There are different approaches used in tarot reading. In most cases, the entire deck is shuffled and cut. During this process, you should think of the question or intention; the tarot spread would then guide the interpretation. You may also opt to use tarot spreads that address specific issues, like relationships and decision-making.

Tarot Spreads Ideal for Beginners

Starting from simple and basic is a great way to build confidence when just learning tarot reading. You may think that being a good tarot reader calls for you to understand and use the ten-card Celtic Cross or twenty or more cards. The good news is that you don't have to master that—at least not yet. In essence, you do not want anything that is too confusing or frustrating you. Take it easy. You can begin by using a single card or a three-card spread for your reading. What is important is your ability to draw meanings from the cards and get insight into what they are saying. Getting connected and intuitive can be particularly challenging when you are overwhelmed and frustrated by your cards.

As you begin, you can adapt one of the various commonly used, simple, and tried tarot spreads. Over time, you can constitute your own tarot spreads.

Single-Card Spread

As the name suggests, you only need one card for your tarot spread. Although it is simple, it is by no means easy because you are relying on one card to give you an adequate interpretation to answer your question. You only need one card to help you answer simple questions that call for a yes or no answer, set the day's tone, or give clarity to life's problems. The catch is also that you do not get a second card or more to clarify. You will be tempted to pull out one card, resist it, and instead, focus all your attention on that one card until the meaning reveals itself.

If you choose to use a single card spread for your

daily reading, you can draw a card and commit it to memory before allowing it to fade into the background. As you go about your day, pay attention to when the card resurfaces into your mind and ask yourself why. At the end of the day, reflect a bit on how the card manifested itself, as well as its meaning.

Alternatively, you can focus on the color of the card you pull out. Determine its meaning and connect to the role it plays in your life and of the people around you.

The single card spread is also a great way to learn your cards. By focusing on a single card, you get to interact with it on an intimate level, giving you a good understanding of its meaning.

Three-Card Tarot Spreads

The three-card tarot spread is ideal for many situations. Aside from it being a classic, it is adaptable to many questions. On top of that, you get adequate information to deliver deep insights without overwhelming yourself. Even seasoned tarot readers opt for this spread.

Here are some three-card spreads you can use.

- **Past-Present-Future Tarot Spreads**

In this spread, the first card you pull represents past elements that have an effect on the future. For instance, if you get a Minor Arcana card like one in the Cups suit, you know the focus is on feelings.

The second card you pull goes to the middle of the line-up and expresses the nature of the question or your current position. A Minor Arcana card here shows that you have control in the situation, whereas a Major Arcana card suggests the need to submit to larger forces in this period.

The third card shows the likely outcome. By meditating on both the past and present cards, you can realise what the card is saying about the future. Even if the future is undesirable, you can make better choices and ease the situation.

- **Mind, Body, and Spirit**

The strength of this tarot spread is in helping you understand what you need to add balance to your life.

The first card is for the body's vitality, flexibility, strength, and health. From it, you can assess the state of your body.

The second card is for the mind and examines its state, including your emotions, repressed feelings, logic, and enlightenment. Here, you also have to pay attention to what brings the body and mind together.

The third card is for your spirit—your subconscious. Here, you look at your instinct, interconnectedness, energy-flow, and intuition. You also need to look at the third card in respect to the first two to help provide clarity and set priorities.

- **Situation-Obstacle-Advice Tarot Spreads**

When faced with a conflict that you need to understand or resolve, this tarot spread is ideal.

The first card is for the situation, and often represents your role.

The second card is for the obstacle and shows the elements that are causing tension or conflict.

The final card is flexible. Although it may reveal a probable outcome, it can also offer advice. The key is to keep an open mind.

- **Blessings-Challenges-Action Tarot Spread**

You can use this tarot spread when dealing with a frustrating situation, or you need clarity about what step to take.

The first card is the blessings card, and as its name suggests, it shows where to find your blessings or what can help in the current situation.

The middle card shows you the challenge; what

you are up against and the problem you have to solve.

The last card is the call for action and indicates what you need to do to address the challenge. You can take this as the answer you seek, and in combination with the blessings card, it can clarify the path to take.

- **No-Spread Tarot Spreads**

In this spread, there is a particular order. You only need to pull out three cards and place them in front of you. The cards support each other and layer the meaning of the overall reading. You can consider each card as a piece of the answer.

- **Nature of Problem-Cause-Solution Tarot Spreads**

Here, the first card gives the nature of the problem be it financial, physical, or emotional.

The second card talks about the cause of the problem.

The third card provides you with the solution to the problem and offers advice on what to do.

• • •

The Clarifying Card

After going through your spread of choice, you may feel the need to clarify. You can pull out a single card to act as the clarifying card; however, you should only do so if your intuition tells you that you need one.

Specialised Tarot Spreads

You may need to use Tarot spreads for different aspects in your life. I will provide you with a few spreads that you can apply to these situations.

Love and Relationships

If there was ever an aspect of life that saw many readings, then it has to be love and relationships. We love to have other people in our lives, but it can start to get blurry when we try to figure out how we should treat them or where the relationship is going. At times in life when you need clarity on a relationship, you can use these three-card tarot spreads.

- **You-Partner-Dynamic**

This is a simple three-card spread that you can use to quickly diagnose the relationship between two people.

With the question in mind, pull out a card and lay it on the left. This card is for you and shows your role in the relationship, the perception you have of yourself, and how that affects the partnership.

Lay the second card on the right, leaving space in the middle for the third card. The second card is for your partner or lover and talks of their role in the relationship, how you perceive them, and how they affect how you relate.

In the middle is where you will place the third card, and this is the one that will give you a description of the relationship, including its characteristics.

• What You Want-What They Want-Where the Relationship is Headed Tarot Spread

You can get answers on how aligned you are in the relationship, while also glimpsing into its future.

The first card you pull in this tarot spread will speak of your relationship expectations, pointing to the needs you wish to fulfill from it.

The second card focuses on what your partner wants from the relationship.

The third card points to where the relationship is going. From the meaning of the card that you have here, you can tell if there is a happily ever after or if it is short-lived.

- **What Unites You-What Draws You Apart-What Needs Attention in Tarot Spread**

For a deeper understanding of your relationship, you can opt for this tarot spread.

The initial card drawn sheds light on the factors that unite and draw you together. These are ones that will make you want to stay in the relationship and make it work. In a way, it is more like the strengths of your relationship.

The next card focuses on the factors that pull you apart and that which could contribute to breaking the relationship. You can take these to be the threats to the stability of the relationship.

The final card depicts the areas in your relationship that need attention. These could be weaknesses or opportunities that you need to explore. Having knowledge in this means you can work at maintaining a strong relationship.

～

Three-Card Tarot Spreads for Making Choices and Decisions

There is certainly something comforting and confidence-boosting about having a sit-down with your deck when faced with a tough decision. To help you get started, here are some tarot spreads you can use for this situation.

- **Strength-Weaknesses- Advice**

Here, the first card shows you what your strengths are, which you can apply in this situation. It reminds you that you do not come empty-handed and have something in you that can work to your advantage.

The next card talks of your weaknesses and can be a good wake-up call for the things you need to be wary of and pits you could fall into.

The third card gives you advice on the best course of action.

- **Option 1-Option2- What to Do Tarot Spread**

Sometimes when you need to make a decision, you may find yourself stuck between two tough choices. At such times, you can consult the card.

Here, the first card gives you an initial option,

while the second card gives you a second one. The third card, however, fills you in with the right information you need to make a good decision.

From this tarot spread, you will receive two choices and pieces of information. It could very well be the light you need to make your life better.

- **Option1-Option 2-Option 3**

For those who would like to have more choices, you can use this tarot spread, which goes beyond giving just two options.

The first card gives you an option, and so do the others. As it is similar to the Option 1-Option 2-What to Do spread, some people consider Option 3 to be the better option. However, the essence of understanding the cards lies in your ability to connect intuitively with them. Look deep within yourself, and you will easily find what the universe is telling you is best.

- **Solution-Alternative Solution-How to Choose Tarot Spread**

Well, if the three options leave you unsure, or you are not the kind of person that likes having many options, then this tarot spread is for you.

The first card will provide you with a solution to your question. The subsequent card also gives you an alternative solution to the first, while the last tells you how to choose the best solution from the two. You can then choose to apply the advice given to pick the best direction to take.

Three-Card Tarot Spreads for Self-Discovery

In life, we are all aiming to become the best versions of ourselves, and we could do this with a little help. That is where tarot cards come in—they give us insights that we can apply in our lives to grow.

∾

Types of Tarot Spreads

Linear Three-Card Tarot Spreads

In a linear spread, the cards suggest a kind of linear path, showing a sequence of events, causes, and effects, or in some instances, how to get from one point to the next.

Some common tarot spreads organized in this way include:

- **Past, Present, Future**—In this spread, there is an interconnected sequence of events from the past to now, and to the future.
- **You, Relationship, Partner**—You and your partner affect your relationship.
- **Situation, Action, Outcome**—The situation you are in determines the course of action you take, which also determines the action. You also need to be in a certain situation to take action and to see the outcome.
- **You, Your Path, Potential**—There is a linear path from you that leads to your path as you edge toward achieving your full potential.
- **Idea, Process, Aspiration**—You need to move from the idea to the implementation process if you are to achieve your aspiration.

Crossed Tarot Spreads

From the name, you can tell that these spreads include conflicts and obstacles. Although people use the three-tarot spread linearly in most cases, you can also opt for a crossed deck. Usually, the card that crosses over signifies something that obstructs one's path, blocking the journey and ultimate success, and it will be the one you need to overcome.

The third card in this spread looks at the situation from a distant perspective, and hence can offer advice on what you need to do.

You may opt to use this kind of a spread with only two cards if you only want the crossing cards.

Some of the cross tarot spreads that you can use here include:

- **Aspiration, Obstacle, How to Overcome** —The obstacle card here crosses over, while the third card sheds light on action to take to overcome the situation.
- **Thesis, Antithesis, Synthesis**—The antithesis card is the one that crosses over, while the synthesis card analyses the situation before offering advice on a proper way out.
- **Opportunities, Challenges, Outcome** —Similarly, the card that crosses over is the

challenges card, while the outcome card gives insight on what to expect, so you can take the best course of action.

- **Situation, Obstacle, Advice**—The second card that crosses over is the one that shows the obstacles before the final card offers advice on how to handle the current situation best.

Balanced Three-Card Tarot Spreads

You can also opt to lay out the cards so there will be a common intersection. The cards in this arrangement are equally important, and without one, the structure will collapse. You can consider them to be the sides of a triangle, each holding its weight. Some examples of these kinds of tarot spreads include:

- **Mind, Body, Spirit**—For you to be whole, these have to work together.
- **Option 1, Option 2, Option 3**—All these options are viable, with none holding more weight than the other.
- **Subconscious, Conscious, and Superconscious**—A holistic person needs to have all three levels of consciousness. These are all crucial.
- **What I Think, How I Feel, What I Do**

—Your thinking, feelings, and actions are all integrated.

- **Physical, Emotional, Spiritual**—All these states are essential parts of life and should be balanced.

Foundational Three-Card Tarot Spreads

The foundational tarot spreads communicate advice in a way that you can understand how one thing relates to the next before giving a final result. You will get a better understanding of options and a summary of how to proceed. Some examples of these spreads include:

- **Strength, Weakness, Advice**—Will help you understand that your strength is this right now, then this is your weakness, take this advice.
- **What Worked, What Did Not, Key Lessons**—You clearly see what worked and what did not, and from that, draw key lessons.
- **What Brings You Together, What Pulls You Apart, What to Work On**—You can see what factors work in your favor, what goes against you, and from these, you can identify what to focus on.

- **Option A, Option B, What You Need to Know to Decide**—Though you have two options, you need this information to help you make the right decision.
- **What You Want, What Your Partner Wants, Where the Relationship Is Heading**—The course of the relationship is dependent on what you and your partner want.

Chapter Summary

In this chapter, we learned that:

- There are different tarot spreads available, from a single card to even ten-card spreads.
- Start small and build up as you get used to tarot reading.
- A three-card tarot spread is most ideal for beginners; it gives depth while not being too overwhelming.

In the next chapter, you will learn how to do a tarot reading by yourself.

CHAPTER 6
TAROT FOR YOU

Despite having all the information, you may still lack the confidence to do a reading for yourself. You are not alone—some people think they cannot read the tarot by themselves, while others are terrified by the thought of some cards telling of their future. To be clear, tarot cards don't predict the future; rather, they tell you what might happen, and of most importance is what you do with that knowledge. There is also the school of thought that suggests it is not right to do a reading for yourself, though that is not true. With enough discipline, preparation, and training, you can read tarot cards.

In this section, I will take you through how to read the tarot for yourself, tap into the energies within yourself to see what is working for or against you. By now, you have probably acquired a deck of your choice and have a good understanding of what the cards mean. That will provide the background. The real power comes from applying your wisdom, tapping into your intuition, and taking positive steps into the future.

~

Designate a Spot

Although many people think that tarot readers perform readings at every other place or any time, that is not true. Most tarot readers have not only a designated space for their reading, but they will often cleanse it to keep it sacred. The cleansing process varies per individual. Some people use water, salt, smoke of palo santo or sage, or even a blend of essential oils, alongside other important accoutrements.

Having a sacred place for your reading will give you a sense of calm and increase your ability to focus.

~

Create the Space

In addition to having an ideal, physical spot designated for tarot reading, it is also important that you create the right environment. Ensure that the space is right, preferably a quiet place, and create the right mood. You can lay out your tarot cloth, burn incense, light a candle, or bring out your favorite crystals.

The emphasis is not only on the physical space, but also the mental. Declutter your mind, take some deep breaths, and relax into it so you can focus on the reading ahead.

The harder part may be creating the ideal emotional space. You should let go of any emotional issues, drama, and hard feelings, and instead, open your mind to the possibility of the cards showing you something new.

You can now set up the spiritual space by establishing an intention for the reading. The time to appeal to the spiritual power is now, so call out to whoever you believe can help you, be it the Universe or angels.

Ask the Question

A crucial step in a tarot reading is asking the cards a question that you seek an answer to. With a clear mind, look within and ask yourself what you need to know. You could look for answers to your relationship, a job opportunity, or anything else that you need clarity on. You must ensure that the question is clear and open-ended for the best results. The essence of using the cards is to illuminate a path and shed light on the future.

Avoid asking questions that lock you into a passive role, such as "Will I...?" Asking such questions assumes that the future is rigid, and there is nothing you can do to change its course. For example, instead of asking, "'ill I land the deal?" you can ask, "How can I improve my chances of landing the deal?" Your questions should be broad to give you better insights into what you are looking for. If you want to have clear and concise answers, you will need to ask a direct question. Vague questions attract equally vague answers.

As a guide, you can structure your questions like this:

- How can I understand...?
- What should I know about...?
- What should I focus on...?
- What am I anxious about...?
- Where is the opportunity in...?

Choose Your Tarot Spread

We have looked at various spreads that you can use in your tarot reading. With a clear question in mind, it is time to choose one, depending on the answers you seek. Remember that there are many different spreads out there, and you need to choose the appropriate one for the question you have in mind.

As a beginner, you may want to keep your tarot spread simple, so you can have good insights and understand what you are reading. Take note of the position of each card to get the right reading. You also do not want to oversimplify the spread; otherwise, you likely won't get much insight.

Shuffle

If you have played any card game, you have most likely shuffled some cards. You can use the overhand shuffle. Here, you will hold the entire deck in one hand and use the other hand to move cards from one side of the deck to the other. Alternatively, you can cut the deck. Divide the cards into several piles, and then combine them again into one. Another way of shuffling is to spread the cards facedown, sweep them into a messy pile, and then tap them into place.

Methods of shuffling vary from one person to the other. Since there is no one acceptable way of shuffling, you can try these methods or even invent your own until you find what works for you.

Shuffling time is a good time to reflect on your question and focus your energy and attention on the cards.

Pull Out a Card

Like shuffling, you can employ whatever method that works for you. You can choose to use the simple approach of cutting the deck and pulling out the top card. Another way of picking a card is to hold the deck in your hand and tilt it slightly to reveal a gap from which you can take a card. Alternatively, you can fan the cards out like in a game of poker, then select a card that feels right.

You can pick the number of cards you need for the chosen tarot spread to answer your question. The more cards picked, the more in-depth the reading will be. As a beginner, it may be best to stick to a small number of cards to avoid feeling overwhelmed.

Read the Cards

After picking the cards, you should lay them face down on the table before turning them up so you can look at their symbols, words, and imagery. The most crucial part of reading is paying attention to how you feel and what comes to mind. Ensure that you stay calm and focus on the cards to connect with your intuitive abilities fully. Do not rush yourself; take your time when connecting with the cards.

Pick each card and analyze them individually.

Look at what it contains and allow the symbols and imagery to guide you toward a meaning. That said, the most important part of the reading is your intuition and how you perceive the message. If you are using more than one card, look at them individually and collectively, so you can connect the meaning as if in a story.

A key point in reading the cards is to study them outside of yourself. Think through the symbols and meanings from a perspective of a second self. By detaching yourself from the reading, you can get better insights that won't be clouded by your thoughts and wishes.

If you are unable to draw any meaning from the cards, come back here for reference or check your deck's reference book.

~

Answer Your Question

Go back to your question and answer it using what the cards have given you. Your study of the cards will have shown you a direction and given you necessary insights. You can use these to provide a straight answer to your questions.

~

Reflect

Some people skip this step, even though it is quite important. You can write down the entire reading, from the questions to the cards drawn, your interpretations, and answers. You can then revisit and reflect on the messages received vis a vis what transpired. What did the cards say and what did you do? Did that land you the deal? From this, you can work on your tarot reading skills as well as confirm your intuition.

Tarot as Self-Care

In these days of hustling and bustling, mindfulness and meditation are important skills. Relax—you can achieve both through tarot card reading. All you need to do is incorporate tarot reading into a regular practice, either daily, weekly, or even monthly. It can also be on a needs basis. Not only will it help you nurture your intuitive abilities, but it will also tap into your inner wisdom. Besides, you will get the answers you seek either on spiritual matters or daily issues.

A simple way of cultivating tarot reading is to draw a card each day, either in the morning or evening that speaks to your day. You can take it as a way of manifesting a better future.

You may not manage to do a proper reading at

first. Do not give up—keep at it. Practice makes perfect.

What to Avoid

Now that you know what to do to have a successful tarot reading for yourself, it is also important to understand the mistakes you should avoid. Look out for some of these things when self-reading.

- **Repeating the same reading**

The cards may not tell you what you need to hear, and we don't like it. There is an impulse to reshuffle the cards, draw again, and see if you can get a more suitable or appealing reading. In some cases, people opt to use the same tarot spread for the same question several times, in an attempt to "challenge" the reading.

Resist the temptation to redo your reading for a different result or confirm the previous one. You will end up muddling the cards, their symbols, and meaning with each new attempt.

- **Reading when highly emotional**

Understandably, the temptation to read when

things are going wrong or too well is usually quite high. However, if you are feeling angry, fearful, pained, or ecstatic, you may want to stay away from the cards. Yes, after a break up or job loss, you shouldn't run straight to the cards... yet.

At such times, you will hardly be in a state of mind that will allow you to reflect with clarity and calmness. Thus, it is best to wait a few days for your emotions to calm down and thoughts to collect. You can take time to reflect on the happening and incident, confront your feelings, and find out what you want to learn from it. By waiting until you are calm and can interact with the cards intuitively, you can then have a successful reading session.

- **Reading cards with your desired outcome in mind**

Often, we want something so bad that we look for signs of it happening everywhere. Similarly, when studying tarot cards, it is important to maintain calm and an open mind. The final interpretation of the tarot cards—no matter the various guides—ultimately depends on the reader. As such, it is best that you can study the cards outside of your biases, emotions, and anxieties.

When you want a certain outcome, you will ignore your intuition and instead opt to twist the meaning of the cards to what you want it to be. The result is that you will start self-guessing and get into a state of confusion between what you perceive to be the meaning and what you think the meaning should be.

For you to read tarot cards successfully, it is best that you always keep an open mind. Trust the cards completely and allow them to lead you to where you should be.

- **The extra card**

You may not repeat the tarot spread, but instead, opt to draw out the extra card. Although it is okay to draw out the extra card when seeking clarity, it is not a good to pick one in the hope of getting answers that affirm your desired outcome. Keep an open and unbiased mind when reading tarot for yourself.

Chapter Summary

You are now ready to do a tarot reading by yourself. All you have to do is:

- Prepare yourself physically, mentally, emotionally, and spiritually, and ask your question.

- Get a suitable deck, shuffle, and pick a card or cards, depending on your tarot spreads.
- Connect intuitively with the cards, analyzing their meaning.
- Answer your question and take time to reflect.
- The most important aspect during a reading is to remain calm and open-minded.

You are now on your way to becoming a great tarot reader. Prepare to receive great insights that will impact your life positively.

CHAPTER 7
FAQS

We have covered what you need to know as a beginner, and I am certain that you are now ready to build
a long-term relationship with your tarot cards. Over
the years, I have noted some of the questions that
people new to tarot reading ask. In this section, I will
address some of these frequently asked questions.

- **Why should I choose tarot?**

Tarot is not only unique and exciting, but it is also a
reflective method of divination. Tarot acts as a mirror
reflecting your inner self back to you in a way that
allows you to get in touch with your deepest feelings.
In addition to helping you clarify the root cause of a
problem you are having, you get a chance to confront

your fears, joys, accomplishments, dreams, and deepest places within you.

- **What can a tarot reading do for me?**

Tarot allows you to look within you, free your intuition, and make the right decisions. Tarot helps you engage with both simple and complex life issues, from everyday tasks like phrasing an email to deep spiritual matters. Besides, you can also use tarot for brainstorming, to spark creativity, progress tracking, and process past experiences. Tarot can also help you map goals, ask questions, and understand your current position in life.

- **What can tarot not do?**

Well, it cannot predict the future perfectly, and there are no guarantees. Tarot is not a substitute for professional medical or legal advice. Also, it will not predict lottery numbers.

- **Does tarot truly predict the future?**

Sometimes the prediction is precise. At other times, it is nuanced or general and only gets detailed over time. Although the future is not cast in stone, every choice and decision takes us toward a destination, making it predictable by divination methods like tarot.

- **Does your first tarot deck have to be gifted?**

You may have heard so, but this is not true. The old traditions came with many superstitions that have now become obsolete. You can go out and buy your first tarot deck if you so choose. If anyone is to get you a deck, then they should let you pick your deck of choice.

- **Should I fear tarot?**

Some people find the insight from tarot reading frightening and its process intimidating, while it is thrilling for others. For most people, the fear emanates from the thought of hearing something negative and the inability to change what they hear. If you are one of those people, take the time to learn more about tarot and embrace it as a great and insightful tool that can offer advice for bettering your life. There is nothing to fear.

- **Is tarot evil?**

Tarot is divine and supernatural. Tarot cards only help you to look deep within. Your interpretations stem from your religious influences, knowledge, and experience, or its lack thereof.

Some people think that since Crowley was evil, so is Thoth tarot. His rival and contemporary, Arthur Waite, on the other hand, was a Christian. The famous Rider Waite tarot deck that is commonly used today has various Christian symbols and emblems. You can, therefore, be certain that tarot cards are not evil.

- **Can I become a tarot reader?**

You may be a beginner now, but yes, you can become not just a tarot reader, but a professional one if you work at it. The first step is to develop interest in tarot reading and get a tarot deck. Read this guide thoroughly, alongside other available resources, like the guide found in your deck. You can also make use of the available online forums. Engage with your cards often so you know them intuitively and can open up to their meanings, rather than through memorization. From here, you can read not only for yourself, but also for others.

• **Can you do a tarot reading online?**

Yes, you can have a reading in person, online, or even over the phone. You may wonder how that works. Through meditation, creating an ideal space, and focusing on the question at hand, you can get the answers you seek from a tarot reader anywhere in the world.

• **What can I ask during a tarot reading?**

Though I am tempted to say you can ask anything, let me narrow my response. Tarot is best for those seeking clarity on issues that cannot be efficiently handled by logic. These tend to be the most important life issues like family matters, negotiations, relationships, and spiritual well-being.

CHAPTER 8
FINAL WORDS

Tarot reading is a reflective and intuitive exercise that allows you to look within you, connect with your inner self, and develop mediation and mindfulness skills. Through tarot reading, you get an opportunity to have some quiet time, ask questions on different aspects of your life, seek answers, and reflect on them. You get a chance to look back at your past, understand where you are now, get a sneak peek into the future, and most importantly take action towards building a better future.

All the goodness that comes with tarot reading is available for everyone. Yes, even that person who is afraid of touching a tarot card can easily grow to become a competent tarot reader. All you need is a deck and some background on the meaning of cards. You do not even need to worry much about this since the interpretation is based more on your intuition and what comes to mind when you see the card. Moreover, the decks come with a guide book that you can use during readings.

After acquisition of a suitable deck, do not be afraid to undertake readings by yourself. You can only improve with practice. The most important thing to remember is that tarot reading needs an open mind and a calm person both emotionally and spiritually. Choose a good place for your readings and focus on the exercise for the best results.

While tarot cards hold information, you hold the power. Nurture and harness that power by undertaking frequent readings. You can start by having a reading each day and build that up. You can also begin by using a single card tarot spread, to three-card spreads and as you learn, you can continually increase the number of cards to have an in depth reading.

Embrace tarot reading for insights into your everyday life or to address deep-seated issues. There is no limit to what you can achieve with an open mind, intuition, and some tarot cards. Start today!

Image Credit: Shutterstock.com

CHAPTER 9
OTHER BOOKS BY THE AUTHOR

Here's a list of books from the author:

1) Wicca for Beginners:

https://www.amazon.com/Wicca-Magic-Complete-Herbal-Fulfill-ebook/dp/B07PN6KLLP

2) Runes for Beginners:

https://www.amazon.com/Runes-Beginners-Complete-Reading-Divination-ebook/dp/B07QDB6NJZ

Lightning Source UK Ltd.
Milton Keynes UK
UKHW020827060223
416538UK00016B/1879